LEITH'S

COOKBOOK

OTHER TITLES IN THE LEITH'S SERIES

Leith's Cookery Bible
Leith's Seasonal Cookery Bible
Leith's Vegetarian Bible

L E I T H ' S

Daily Mail

COOKBOOK

Introduction by Caroline Waldegrave

BLOOMSBURY

First published in Great Britain by Bloomsbury Publishing 2002

All recipes copyright © Leith's School of Food and Wine Ltd
All illustrations copyright © Tess Stone

The moral rights of the authors have been asserted

Bloomsbury Publishing Plc, 38 Soho Square, London W1D 3HB

A CIP catalogue record is available from the British Library

ISBN 0 7475 6147 8

10 9 8 7 6 5 4 3 2 1

Typeset by Hewer Text Ltd, Edinburgh
Printed in Great Britain by Clays Ltd, St Ives plc

CONTENTS

CONTRIBUTORS

Viv Pidgeon
Max Clark
Caroline Waldegrave
Jenny Gillison
Kat Vanderpump
Belinda Spinney
Sue Spaull
Sue Brown
Puff Fairclough
Priya Wickramasinghe
Victoria Fry
Fiona Burell
Sara Blount
Jane Nemazee
CJ Jackson
Eithne Neame
Polly Tyrer
Valeria Sisti
Janey Orr
Anne Heughan

INTRODUCTION

At Leith's School we run a regular course called Easy Dinner-Party Cooking which is always very popular. This course is quite a departure for us, in that it includes quick and easy cooking methods and the use of some convenience foods. Throughout the rest of the year we are purists: we make all our own stocks and pastries, fillet our fish and butcher our meat; we don't acknowledge the existence of a jar of pesto sauce or contemplate buying ready-made pasta. So the dinner-party course is our moment of freedom, when we finally own up to what we do at home after a busy day at work – we all enjoy cooking 'real' food at the weekends but often have no time during the week so we shop at the supermarket on the way home.

One year, Susie Dowdall from the *Daily Mail* joined us on the dinner-party course and we discussed the idea of publishing a recipe for an easy dish on a daily basis in the newspaper. It didn't take long for the idea to become reality. We were given a fairly strict brief: the recipes had to be pretty much skill-free – for example, no gelatine, no whisking egg whites, no pastry-making and no complicated sauces; we were told that *Daily Mail* readers like soups, fish, cakes and biscuits. To begin with we stuck rigidly to the brief, but after a year we began to introduce a few skills. Essentially, though, the recipes remain easy, delicious, quick to make and suitable for supper or dinner parties. The ideas are suitable for either last-minute cooking or to be prepared in advance and frozen or reheated as required.

The recipes have been written by a large number of the teachers at Leith's. Someone will have an initial idea for a dish, the recipe

1

for which is then tested. With testing completed, I will write an introduction offering as much practical advice as possible for reheating instructions, serving suggestions and catering quantities. Tested recipes being tasted constantly interrupt life in the office at the school – many prospective students have been offered dishes to taste mid-interview.

During the testing process we have become increasingly aware of the array of convenience foods now available in good-quality supermarkets.

The manufacturing process generally makes it more expensive to buy convenience food than to cook from scratch, but the cost has to be balanced against the value of your time – this in itself makes convenience food the preferable option to some.

However, it is easy to get carried away with ready-prepared foods. Some are completely pointless – ready-cut vegetables, for example, which are invariably dried out and have lost most of their nutritional value – while others, such as powdered mashed potato, just don't seem to taste like the real thing. On the whole, cans and jars are better than dried mixes requiring reconstitution. The quantities called for in the recipes are generally standard supermark pack sizes and can be varied slightly depending on availability.

While writing these recipes we have gradually compiled the following list of items that work well:

Pastry: puff, shortcrust, filo
Tempura-batter mix
Ready-made pancakes
Dried and fresh pasta
Organic tomato sauces or passata (not tomato pasta sauces)
Hollandaise in jars
Canned pulses
Croissant dough
Pizza-base mixes (not ready-made pizza bases)
Good-quality ice cream

INTRODUCTION

Fresh or concentrated liquid stock or bouillon (not cubes)
Par-cooked risotto
Par-cooked couscous
Curry pastes (not powders)
Pestos
Tapenades
Good quality mayonnaise

I was very pleased when a suggestion was made to publish our favourite recipes of the last 2 years – and I know that some regular readers were desperate for the book to be published as their cutting collections had got out of hand. I have enjoyed the trip down memory lane and I hope that you enjoy cooking from these recipes. I would particularly like to thank Liz Rowlinson at the *Daily Mail* for all her help in producing the recipes on time.

Caroline Waldegrave

3

CATERING QUANTITIES

Few people accurately weigh or measure quantities as a control-conscious chef must do, but when catering for large numbers it is useful to know how much food to allow per person. As a general rule, the more you are catering for the less food per head you need to provide, e.g. 225g/8oz stewing beef per head is essential for 4 people, but 170g/6oz per head would feed 60 people. The following quantities are fairly generous.

Soup
Allow 290ml/½ pint soup per head, depending on the size of the bowl.

Poultry
Chicken Allow 340g/12oz per person, weighed when plucked and drawn. An average chicken serves 4 people on the bone and 6 people off the bone.

Duck A 2.7kg/6lb bird will feed 3–4 people; a 1.8kg/4lb bird will feed 2 people. 1 duck makes enough pâté for 6 people.

Goose Allow 3.6kg/8lb for 4 people; 6.9kg/15lb for 7 people.

Turkey Allow 450g/1lb on the bone per person, weighed when plucked and drawn – i.e. a 6.9kg/15lb bird will feed 15 people.

Game
Pheasant Allow 1 bird for 2 people (roast); 1 bird for 3 people (casseroled).

Pigeon Allow 1 bird per person.

Grouse Allow 1 young grouse per person (roast); 1 bird for 2–3 people (casseroled).

Quail Allow 2 small birds per person or 1 large boned stuffed bird served on a croûte.

Partridge Allow 1 bird per person.

Venison Allow 170g/6oz lean meat per person; 1.8kg/4lb cut of haunch weighed on the bone for 8–9 people.

Steaks Allow 170–225g/6–8oz per person.

Meat

Lamb or Mutton

Casseroled 225g/8oz boneless trimmed meat per person.

Roast leg 1.35kg/3lb for 3–4 people; 1.8kg/4lb for 4–5 people; 2.7kg/6lb for 7–8 people.

Roast shoulder 1.8kg/4lb shoulder for 5–6 people; 2.7kg/6lb shoulder for 7–9 people.

Grilled best end cutlets 3–4 per person.

Grilled loin chops 2 per person.

Beef

Stewed 225g/8oz boneless trimmed meat per person.

Roast (off the bone) If serving men only, 225g/8oz per person; if serving men and women, 200g/7oz per person.

Roast (on the bone) 340g/12oz piece per person.

Roast whole fillet 1.8kg/4lb piece for 10 people.

Grilled steaks 170–225g/6–7oz per person.

Pork

Casseroled 170g/6oz per person.

Roast leg or loin (off the bone) 200g/7oz per person.

Roast leg or loin (on the bone) 340g/12oz per person.

2 average fillets will feed 3–4 people.

Grilled 1 × 170g/6oz chop or cutlet per person.

Veal
Stews or pies 225g/8oz pie veal per person.
Fried 1 × 170g/6oz escalope per person.

Minced Meat
170g/6oz per person for shepherd's pie, hamburgers, etc.
110g/4oz per person for steak tartare.
85g/3oz per person for lasagne, cannelloni, etc.
110g/4oz per person for moussaka.
55g/2oz per person for spaghetti.

Fish
Whole large fish (e.g. sea bass, salmon, whole haddock), weighed
unclean, with head on: 340–450g/12oz–1lb per person.
Cutlets and steaks 170g/6oz per person
Fillets (e.g. sole, lemon sole, plaice): 3 fillets per person.
Whole small fish (e.g. trout, slip soles, small plaice, small mackerel,
herring) 225–340g/8–12oz weighed with heads for main course;
170g/6oz for first course.
Fish off the bone (in fish pie, with sauce, etc.) 170g/6oz per person.

Shellfish
Prawns 55–85g/2–3oz per person as a first course; 140g/5oz per
person as a main course.
Mixed shellfish 55–85g/2–3oz per person as a first course;
140g/5oz per person as a main course.

Vegetables
Weighed before preparation and cooking, and assuming 3 vege-
tables, including potatoes, served with a main course: 110g/4oz per
person, except (per person):
French beans 55g/2oz.
Peas 55g/2oz.
Spinach 340g/12oz.

Potatoes 3 small (roast); 170g/6oz (mashed); 1 large or 2 small (baked); 110g/4oz (new).

Rice
Plain, boiled or fried 55g/2oz (weighed before cooking).
In risotto or pilaf 30g/1oz per person (weighed before cooking) for first course; 55g/2oz per person for main course.

Salads
Obviously, the more salads served, the less guests will eat of any one salad. Allow 1–1½ portions of salad, in total, per head – e.g. if only one salad is served make sure there is enough for 1 generous helping each. Conversely if 100 guests are to choose from 5 different salads, allow a total of 150 portions – i.e. 30 portions of each salad.
Tomato salad 450g/1lb tomatoes (average 6 tomatoes), sliced, serves 4 people.
Coleslaw 1 small cabbage, finely shredded, serves 10–12 people.
Grated carrot salad 450g/1lb carrots, grated, serves 6 people.
Potato salad 450g/1lb potatoes (weighed before cooking) serves 5 people.
Green salad Allow a loose handful of leaves for each person.

Sandwiches
2 slices of bread make 1 round of sandwiches.
Cucumber 1 cucumber makes 15 rounds.
Egg 1 hard-boiled egg makes 1 round.
Ham Allow 20g/¾oz for each round.
Mustard and cress For egg and cress sandwiches, 1 punnet makes 20 rounds.
Tomato 450g/1lb makes 9 rounds
Smoked salmon Allow 20g/¾oz for each round.

Cocktail Parties
Allow 10 cocktail canapés per head

Allow 14 cocktail canapés per head if served at lunchtime when guests are unlikely to go on to a meal.

Allow 4–5 cocktail canapés with pre-lunch or pre-dinner drinks.

Allow 8 cocktail canapés plus 4 miniature sweet cakes or pastries per head for a wedding reception.

Miscellaneous

Brown bread and butter 1½ slices (3 triangular pieces) per person.

French bread 1 large loaf for 8 people; 1 small loaf for 4 people.

Cheese After a meal, if serving one blue-veined, one hard and one soft cheese: 85g/3oz per person for up to 8 people; 55g/2oz per person for over 20 people.

At a wine and cheese party: 110g/4oz per person for up to 8 people; 85g/3oz per person for up to 20 people; 55g/2oz per person for over 20 people. Inevitably, if catering for small numbers, there will be cheese left over but this is unavoidable if the host is not to look mean.

Biscuits 3 each for up to 10 people; 2 each for up to 30 people; 1 each for over 30 people.

Butter 30g/1oz per person if bread is served with the meal; 45g/1½oz per person if cheese is served as well. 30g/1oz soft butter will cover 8 large bread slices.

Cream 1 tablespoon per person for coffee, 3 tablespoons per person for pudding or dessert.

Milk 570ml/1 pint for 18–20 cups of tea.

Sliced bread A large loaf, thinly sliced, generally makes 18–20 slices.

Sausages 450g/1lb is the equivalent of 32 cocktail sausages; 16 chipolata sausages; 8 pork sausages.

Chicken livers 450g/1lb chicken livers will be enough for 60 bacon and chicken liver rolls.

Dates 50 fresh dates weigh about 450g/1lb.

Prunes A prune (with stone) weighs about 10g/⅓oz.

Mushrooms A button mushroom weighs about 7g/¼oz.

Bacon A good-sized rasher weighs about 30g/1oz.

CATERING QUANTITIES

Button onions A button onion weighs about 15g/½oz.
Choux pastry 6-egg choux paste makes 150 baby éclairs. They will
need 570ml/1 pint cream for filling and 225g/8oz chocolate for
coating.
Short pastry 900g/2lb pastry will line 150 tartlets.

EASY DINNER-PARTY ADVICE

It is important to be able to enjoy the evening, so here are a few simple guidelines to make things easier:

- *Mise-en-place* (prepare in advance). Leave yourself plenty of time for preparation, on the evening of the night before – even laying the table can help. Choose dishes that can be prepared all or part of the way through in advance. Don't be too proud to stick to a plan of action on the wall and follow it slavishly – professional cooks do it all the time and it saves their sanity and a lot of time.
- A cold first course or pudding (or both) makes life easier.
- Do not cook too many types of vegetables. One or two cooked beautifully is much better than a huge variety overcooked or kept warm for too long. Blanch and refresh your vegetables in advance. They can be reheated in a microwave or plunged into boiling water just before serving.
- Do not attempt new dishes/methods. Practise first on unsuspecting partners or friends.
- Portion control. Individual tarts, puddings, etc., look better for presentation and are easier to plate. Also, it is clear how many you have.
- Do any 'smelly' cooking before your guests arrive (chargrilling, frying, etc.). You and your kitchen do not want to smell of food when they arrive.
- Do not worry. Good ingredients and preparation speak for themselves.
- Think about presentation before you start serving. Make sure

you know how you would like the food to look in advance. (See notes on food presentation, pages 12–14.)
- Plan your menu carefully (see notes).

Menu Planning

The most obvious but important rule must be to keep things simple. There is no point in attempting so much that the quality of execution is threatened. Don't try to be too clever.

There are several things to bear in mind when planning a menu:

- **Season of the year: hot or cold** Although delicious, hearty soups such as smoked haddock chowder should probably be kept for a winter menu while cucumber soup can be served for a summer one.
- **Availability of ingredients and seasonal constraints** For example, baked peaches and strawberry cream will really only work in the summer.
- **Cost/budget** Entertaining needn't be prohibitively expensive – choosing recipes wisely, with ingredients that you already have in your store cupboard and/or that are in season, makes a cost-effective way of seeing friends.
- **Type of people** If you are cooking for old-fashioned friends we would not recommend giving them exotic or unusual ingredients.
- **Special diets** The most obvious example of this is vegetarian.
- **Style of occasion** The menu you plan for a special birthday will be quite different to the one that you serve for an informal light supper.
- **Size and equipment of kitchen**
- **Size and equipment of dining area**
- **Holding ability** If you are short of time or want to prepare ahead, choosing a cold starter or pudding is sensible.
- **Balancing a menu** If a menu isn't properly balanced your guests can feel bloated and over-full. The most common mistake is to provide too much rich food. The secret is not

11

to abandon creamy or buttery dishes but to limit their size and number. The main thing to aim for is plenty of fresh fruit and vegetables, some starch, but not too many fatty or meaty foods.

Avoid repetition of:

Ingredients e.g. tomato salad followed by lamb steaks with tomatoes and butterbeans.

Check that the first or main course and the pudding are not predominantly fruit – e.g. melon to start, meat, poultry or fish with a fruity sauce and fruit salad to finish.

Colours e.g. a meal of parsnip soup, smoked haddock rarebit with mashed potato, then bread and butter pudding provides no variation in colour and would not look very attractive. Also think about the colour of your main-course plates and what you are serving on them.

Method of cooking e.g. seared tuna followed by chargrilled lamb.

Words e.g. roast tomatoes, roast lamb with roast vegetables.

Texture If the main course is a tender casserole served with mashed potatoes to mop up the gravy, provide something crunchy such as crisp French beans to go with it. Some cooks have found their food processors hard to resist and the result can be smooth pâté, followed by lasagne, followed by a custard pudding, so that guests quite literally long for something they can get their teeth into.

Food Presentation

If food looks delicious, people are predisposed to find that it tastes delicious too. If you have spent time organising, preparing and cooking your meal, it seems a shame to just dump the food on a plate. At Leith's School we have gradually developed a set of rules which can be used as guidelines when presenting food. Fashion may dictate the method – be it stylish, nouvelle cuisine or chunky real food – but the guidelines are the same. The following is a summary:

- **Keep it simple** Over-decorated food often looks messed about – no longer appetising but like an uncertain work of art. The more cluttered the plate, the less attractive it inevitably becomes.
- **Keep it fresh** Nothing looks more off-putting than tired food. Sprigs of herbs used for garnish should always be absolutely fresh; pot herbs, now widely available in supermarkets, make this easy to achieve. Salad wilts when dressed in advance, deep-fried or sautéed food can become dull and dry when kept warm for hours, and whipped cream goes buttery in a warm room – so don't risk it.
- **Decorating and garnishing** This can completely alter the final look of a dish. The ultimate aim is to 'bring the dish together'. A dusting of icing sugar over a pudding or a garnish of dill with a salmon cutlet are relatively simple and inexpensive additions to the cost of a dish but will certainly increase the expectation and enjoyment.
- **Keep it relevant** A sprig of watercress complements lamb cutlets nicely – the texture, taste and colour all do something for the dish – but scratchy sprigs of parsley, though they may provide colour, are unpleasant to eat. Tomato slices do not improve the look of a platter of sandwiches – they serve simply to distract and confuse the eye.
- **Centre height** Dishes served on platters are best given 'centre height' – arranged so that the mound of food is higher in the middle with the sides sloping down. Coat carefully and evenly with the sauce, if any. Do not overload serving platters with food, as this makes serving difficult.
- **Limit the number of colours** As with any design, it is easier to get a pleasing effect if the colours are controlled – say, just green or white.
- **Contrast the simple and the elaborate** If the dish or bowl is elaborately decorated, contrasting simple foods tends to show it off better. Conversely a plain white plate sets off pretty food design to perfection.

13

- **Overlapping** Chops, steaks, sliced meats and even rashers of bacon look best evenly overlapping. This way more of them can be fitted comfortably on the serving dish than if placed side by side, and the dish is given some height.
- **Best side uppermost** Usually the side of a steak or cutlet that is grilled or fried first looks the best and should be placed uppermost. Bones are generally unsightly and should be tucked out of the way.
- **Individual plating** Until the advent of nouvelle cuisine in the 1970s it was considered a caterer's short-cut trick to plate dishes individually, then suddenly it became the only way to present food. But now, with the advent of a more rustic or family approach to food and cooking, we are returning to food served at the table from the dish in which it was cooked. However, at special occasions plating food still seems smarter and the usual presentation rules apply. Keep it simple and relevant.
- **How much to serve** A daunting plateful tends to take away the appetite, so do not overload plates. Take trouble to arrange things neatly and attractively on the plate. Slops and drips look bad, so take time when spooning a sauce to let any excess run off the spoon before moving away from the main serving dish to the plate.

CONVERSION TABLES

The tables below are approximate, and do not conform in all respects to the conventional conversions, but we have found them convenient for cooking. Use either metric or imperial measurements: do not mix the two.

Weight

Imperial	Metric	Imperial	Metric
¼oz	7–8g	½oz	15g
¾oz	20g	1oz	30g
2oz	55g	3oz	85g
4oz (¼lb)	110g	5oz	140g
6oz	170g	7oz	200g
8oz (½lb)	225g	9oz	255g
10oz	285g	11oz	310g
12oz (¾lb)	340g	13oz	370g
14oz	400g	15oz	425g
16oz (1lb)	450g	1¼lb	560g
1½lb	675g	2lb	900g
3lb	1.35kg	4lb	1.8kg
5lb	2.3kg	6lb	2.7kg
7lb	3.2kg	8lb	3.6kg
9lb	4.0kg	10lb	4.5kg

Australian cup measures

	Metric	Imperial
1 cup flour	140g	5oz
1 cup sugar (crystal or caster)	225g	8oz
1 cup brown sugar, firmly packed	170g	6oz
1 cup icing sugar, sifted	170g	6oz
1 cup butter	225g	8oz
1 cup honey, golden syrup, treacle	370g	12oz
1 cup fresh breadcrumbs	55g	2oz
1 cup packaged dry breadcrumbs	140g	5oz
1 cup crushed biscuit crumbs	110g	4oz
1 cup rice, uncooked	200g	7oz
1 cup mixed fruit or individual fruit, such as sultanas	170g	6oz
1 cup nuts, chopped	110g	4oz
1 cup coconut, desiccated	85g	3oz

Approximate American/European conversions

Commodity	USA	Metric	Imperial
Flour	1 cup	140g	5oz
Caster and granulated sugar	1 cup	225g	8oz
Caster and granulated sugar	2 level tablespoons	30g	1oz
Brown sugar	1 cup	170g	6oz
Butter/margarine/lard	1 cup	225g	8oz
Sultanas/raisins	1 cup	200g	7oz
Currants	1 cup	140g	5oz
Ground almonds	1 cup	110g	4oz
Golden syrup	1 cup	340g	12oz
Uncooked rice	1 cup	200g	7oz
Grated cheese	1 cup	110g	4oz
Butter	1 stick	110g	4oz

Liquid measures

Imperial	ml	fl oz
1 teaspoon	5	
2 scant tablespoons	28	1
4 scant tablespoons	56	2
¼ pint (1 gill)	150	5
⅓ pint	190	6.6
½ pint	290	10
¾ pint	425	15
1 pint	570	20
1¾ pints	1000 (1 litre)	35

Australian

250ml	1 cup
20ml	1 tablespoon
5ml	1 teaspoon

Approximate American/European conversions

American	European
1 teaspoon	1 teaspoon/5ml
½fl oz	1 tablespoon/½fl oz/15ml
¼ cup	4 tablespoons/2fl oz/56ml
½ cup plus 2 tablespoons	¼ pint/5fl oz/150ml
1¼ cups	½ pint/10fl oz/290ml
1 pint/16fl oz	1 pint/20fl oz/570ml
2½ pints (5 cups)	1.1 litres/2 pints
10 pints	4.5 litres/8 pints

Useful measurements

Measurement	Metric	Imperial
1 American cup	225ml	8fl oz
1 egg, medium	56ml	2fl oz
1 egg white	28ml	1fl oz
1 rounded tablespoon flour	30g	1oz
1 rounded tablespoon cornflour	30g	1oz
1 rounded tablespoon caster sugar	30g	1oz
2 rounded tablespoons fresh breadcrumbs	30g	1oz
2 level teaspoons gelatine	8g	¼oz

30g/1oz granular (packet) aspic sets
570ml/1 pint liquid.

15g/½ oz powdered gelatine, or 4 leaves, will set 570ml/1 pint liquid. (However, in hot
weather, or if the liquid is very acid, like lemon juice, or if the jelly contains solid pieces of
food and is to be turned out of the dish or mould, 20g/¾oz should be used.)

CONVERSION TABLES

Wine quantities

Imperial	ml	fl oz
Average wine bottle	750	25
1 glass wine	100	3½
1 glass port or sherry	70	2
1 glass liqueur	45	1

Lengths

Imperial	Metric
½in	1cm
1in	2.5cm
2in	5cm
6in	15cm
12in	30cm

Oven temperatures

°C	°F	Gas mark	AMERICAN	AUSTRALIAN
70	150	¼		
80	175	¼	COOL	VERY SLOW
100	200	½		
110	225	½		
130	250	1	VERY SLOW	
140	275	1		SLOW
150	300	2	SLOW	
170	325	3	MODERATE	MODERATELY SLOW
180	350	4		
190	375	5	MODERATELY HOT	MODERATE
200	400	6	FAIRLY HOT	
220	425	7	HOT	MODERATELY HOT
230	450	8	VERY HOT	
240	475	8		HOT
250	500	9		
270	525	9	EXTREMELY HOT	VERY HOT
290	550	9		

FOOD SAFETY

These are the most important factors to take into account for food safety.

1. Bugs like warmth, moisture and to be left undisturbed, so try not to give them these ideal conditions.
2. Keep cooking utensils and hands clean. Change J-cloths, tea towels and washing-up brushes regularly.
3. Store raw meat at the bottom of the refrigerator, so that any meat juices cannot drip on to cooked food. Place raw meat on a tray with a lip.
4. Wrap food up loosely, let it breathe.
5. Don't put hot food into the refrigerator – it will raise the temperature. Refrigerators should be kept at 5°C.
6. Get food to cool down as quickly as possible.
7. Never cover cooling hot food.
8. Avoid cross-contamination of germs – store raw and cooked foods separately as far as possible. If you mix raw and cooked foods they should both be cold and then reheated thoroughly. Avoid keeping food warm for any length of time: it should be either hot or cold.
9. Never cook large items (e.g. whole chickens) from frozen.
10. Salmonella in eggs: consumption of raw eggs or uncooked dishes made from them, such as home-made mayonnaise, mousse and ice cream, carries the risk of food poisoning. If you do use raw eggs, make sure that you use only the freshest (pasteurised eggs are available), that the dishes are eaten as soon as possible after making and that they are never left for

more than 1 hour at room temperature.

Vulnerable people such as the elderly, the sick, babies, toddlers and pregnant women should only eat eggs that have been thoroughly cooked until both white and yolk are solid. Eggs that have the lion quality mark are guaranteed to have come from hens vaccinated against Salmonella. Pasturised eggs are also available in some supermarkets.

SOUPS

CREAM OF CELERY SOUP WITH STILTON CROÛTES

This delicious, warming soup is ideal as a complete meal in itself. The croûtes complement the soup perfectly, but are very rich and should probably be omitted if you are serving the soup as the first course of a three-course meal. The soup can be made in advance to the end of stage 3 and then frozen or reheated as required.

Preparation time: 20 minutes
Cooking time: 40 minutes
Serves 4

45g/1½oz butter
1 leek, very finely chopped
1 celery head, cleaned and very
  finely sliced (reserve the tops)
2 tablespoons water
salt and freshly ground white
  pepper
290ml/½ pint vegetable stock or
  water
290ml/½ pint full-cream milk
4 tablespoons double cream

For the croûtes
1 small baguette, split
  horizontally and toasted
55g/2oz Stilton, crumbled
1 tablespoon crème fraîche

To garnish
celery leaves

1. Melt the butter in a large saucepan. Add the leek, celery and water and season with salt and pepper. Cover with a tight-fitting lid and cook over a very low heat for 20–25 minutes or until soft but not coloured.
2. Add the vegetable stock or water, bring to the boil and simmer gently for

10 minutes. Remove from the heat. Liquidise in a food processor or blender and pass through a fine sieve into the rinsed-out saucepan.

3. Add the milk and double cream and heat through gently without boiling.

4. Meanwhile, mix together the Stilton and crème fraîche and spread over the cut side of the toasted baguette halves. Grill until the cheese bubbles, then cut each half into 4 pieces.

5. Divide the croûtes between 4 soup bowls. Carefully ladle the hot soup over the croûtes and serve garnished with the celery leaves.

SMOKED HADDOCK CHOWDER

This soup is very easy to make and can be prepared in advance and then frozen or reheated as required. Try to buy good-quality smoked haddock – it has a better flavour than the very yellow, dyed variety and is generally less salty.

Preparation time: 20 minutes
Cooking time: 30 minutes
Serves 4

30g/1oz butter
1 large onion, chopped
110g/4oz bacon lardons
1 large potato peeled and cut into chunks
425ml/¾ pint fish stock, or water
150ml/¼ pint milk

150ml/¼ pint double cream or crème fraîche
340g/12oz skinned smoked haddock, cut into pieces
55g/2oz peas, fresh or frozen
salt and freshly ground black pepper

1. Melt the butter in a large saucepan and sweat the onions over a low heat.

2. Add the bacon and cook until golden in colour.

3. Add the potatoes and stock and bring to the boil. Simmer until the potatoes are tender.

4. Add the milk and cream and bring to a gentle simmer. Add the haddock and peas and continue to cook until the haddock is cooked through, but try not to stir too much or the fish will break up.

5. Taste and season with salt and pepper. Serve immediately.

ROAST RED ONION AND CARROT SOUP

This simple and delicious soup is satisfying enough to serve as a main course for lunch yet is very low in fat. It can be made well in advance and then frozen or reheated as required.

Preparation time: 5 minutes
Cooking time: 1 hour
Serves 4

2 tablespoons oil
3 red onions, cut into wedges
6 medium carrots, peeled and cut
  into chunks
salt and freshly ground black
  pepper
2 bay leaves

1 sprig of thyme
860ml/1½ pints vegetable stock
  or water

To garnish
chives or sprigs of chervil

1. Preheat the oven to 200°C/400°F/gas mark 6.
2. Heat the oil in a roasting pan large enough to take the vegetables in one layer.
3. Place the onions and carrots in the roasting pan and turn carefully in the hot oil. Season with salt and black pepper.
4. Add the bay leaves and thyme to the pan and roast, turning occasionally, for 30–45 minutes or until the vegetables are tender and beginning to caramelise. Transfer to a saucepan.
5. Add the stock or water to the pan and bring to the boil, reduce the heat to a simmer and cook for a further 10–15 minutes.
6. Remove the bay leaves and thyme and liquidise the soup in a food processor or blender. Pass through a sieve into the rinsed-out saucepan and bring to the boil. Season to taste and serve garnished with the chives or sprigs of chervil.

LENTIL SOUP

This is an easy soup to make and can be cooked in advance and then reheated or frozen as required. If the lentils can be cooked in a pressure cooker, they will be cooked in 3 minutes.

Preparation time: 5 minutes
Cooking time: 20 minutes
Serves 4–6

1 small onion, finely chopped
1 carrot, finely chopped
1 × 500g/1¼lb packet orange lentils, rinsed
1.14–1.4l/2–2½ pints water
2 × 130g/4½oz packets ready-chopped pancetta

2 tablespoons crème fraîche (optional)
salt and freshly ground pepper

To garnish
chopped parsley

1. Put the onion, carrot, lentils and 1.14l/2 pints of the water into a heavy saucepan. Bring slowly to the boil, skimming away scum as it rises to the surface. Season with salt and pepper.
2. Simmer for 10–20 minutes, or until the lentils are very soft indeed. Add extra water if the soup seems very thick. Stir vigorously to pulverise the lentils, then taste and add extra salt and pepper if necessary.
3. Meanwhile, fry the pancetta in a hot frying pan until lightly browned all over. Drain well on absorbent paper and add to the soup.
4. Add the crème fraîche and serve in warm soup bowls garnished with a little chopped parsley.

CARROT AND CORIANDER SOUP

This soup is quick and easy to make. Its colour makes it attractive to children and the coriander adds a touch of sophistication, which means that it is popular with adults and suitable for family cooking and dinner parties alike. The soup can be prepared in advance and then reheated or frozen as required.

Preparation time: 5 minutes
Cooking time: 45 minutes
Serves 4

*675g/1½lb carrots, peeled and
    sliced*
1 onion, finely chopped
15g/½oz butter
1 bay leaf
*860ml/1½ pints white stock or
    water*
*salt and freshly ground black
    pepper*
*1 tablespoon chopped fresh
    parsley*
*1 tablespoon chopped fresh
    coriander*
4 tablespoons double cream

1. Put the carrots and onion into a large heavy saucepan with the butter. Sweat for 10 minutes or until the vegetables begin to soften. Add the bay leaf, stock, salt and pepper. Bring to the boil, then simmer as slowly as possible for 25 minutes. Remove the bay leaf.
2. Remove from the heat. Liquidise the soup with the parsley and coriander in a food processor or blender and push through a sieve into a clean saucepan. Check the consistency. If too thin, reduce by rapid boiling; if too thick, add extra water.
3. Add the cream and season to taste with salt and pepper.

MINTED PEA AND CUCUMBER SOUP

This refreshing cold soup can be made with fresh garden peas or frozen petits pois. Don't bother to defrost the peas – just add them to the hot stock and cook as directed. Adding a pinch of sugar when cooking peas helps to bring out their natural sweetness. Serve the soup with crusty wholemeal bread and some cheese for a light summer lunch or as a first course for a dinner party. The soup can be made a day in advance if kept chilled in the fridge.

Preparation time: 10 minutes
Cooking time: 20 minutes
Serves 4

1 tablespoon olive oil
1 small onion, chopped
110g/4oz floury potato, peeled
  and grated
570ml/1 pint chicken or vegetable
  stock
salt and freshly ground black pepper
250g/9oz small garden peas

pinch of sugar
½ cucumber, peeled and deseeded
85ml/3fl oz double cream
1 tablespoon chopped fresh mint
  leaves (reserve the stalks)

To garnish
4 sprigs mint

1. Place the oil in a small saucepan and stir in the onion. Cook over a low heat until softened.
2. Add the potato, stock and mint stalks and bring to the boil. Stir in the peas with a pinch of sugar, then simmer for 20 minutes or until the vegetables have softened.
3. Finely dice the cucumber, salt lightly, then place in a sieve to drain.
4. Allow the soup to cool, then remove the mint stalks. Purée in a food processor or blender, then pass through a sieve into a clean saucepan.
5. Stir in the cucumber, cream and chopped mint. Season as required.
6. Chill well before serving garnished with the mint sprigs.

MEXICAN BEAN SOUP

This delicious and beautifully coloured soup can be served as a first course or as a main course with plenty of crusty bread. Soured cream can be used as an alternative garnish to the crisps.

Preparation time: 15 minutes
Cooking time: 20 minutes
Serves 4–6

1 tablespoon oil
1 onion, roughly chopped
1 red chilli, finely chopped
1 clove garlic, crushed
1 × 450g/1lb can peeled chopped
  tomatoes
pinch of sugar
1 × 450g/1lb can cooked mixed
  beans, drained and rinsed

425ml/¾ pint chicken or
  vegetable stock
salt and freshly ground black
  pepper

To serve
grated cheese
tortilla crisps
1 tablespoon chopped fresh
  coriander

1. Heat the oil in a heavy-based pan. Add the onion and cook until it begins to soften. Add the chilli and continue to cook for 2 minutes, then add the garlic and cook for 1 more minute.
2. Add the tomatoes, sugar and beans to the onions and heat through. Add the stock, bring to the boil and simmer for 5 minutes. Season to taste with salt and pepper.
3. Serve in warmed bowls, topped with grated cheese, a couple of tortilla crisps and fresh coriander.

CUCUMBER AND MELON GAZPACHO

This is almost my favourite summer soup – it is very easy to make yet tastes subtle and sophisticated. It is ideal for a summer dinner party (hence the quantity). It may need to be liquidised in several batches. A blender will give a much smoother finish than a food processor. It can be made a day in advance but does not freeze well.

Preparation time: 20 minutes
Serves 6–8

*2 large cucumbers, peeled and
    deseeded
1 medium Galia melon, peeled
    and deseeded
1 bunch of rocket
3 sprigs fresh dill
3 sprigs fresh mint
2 tablespoons tarragon vinegar
1 small clove garlic, peeled
1 small green chilli, deseeded*

*290ml/½ pint carrot juice or
    mixed vegetable juice
150ml/¼ pint Greek yoghurt
6 tablespoons olive oil
salt and freshly ground black
    pepper*

*To garnish
crushed ice
sprigs fresh dill*

1. Finely dice ¼ of 1 cucumber and 1 slice of melon. Reserve.
2. Chop the remaining cucumber and melon roughly and put into a food processor or blender with the rocket, dill, mint, vinegar, garlic, chilli and half the carrot or mixed vegetable juice. Liquidise to a smooth paste and gradually blend in the remaining juice, yoghurt and oil. Season to taste with the salt and pepper. Refrigerate until cold.
3. Pour into 6 individual soup bowls and garnish with the reserved cucumber and melon, crushed ice and sprigs of dill.

BUTTERNUT SQUASH AND THYME SOUP

Butternut squash makes excellent soup – its natural sweetness means that it is popular with children and its smooth texture gives the finished soup a velvet finish. This soup can be made in advance and then frozen or reheated as required. If making the soup for vegetarians, use vegetable stock or water in place of the chicken stock.

Preparation time: 5–6 minutes
Cooking time: 40 minutes
Serves 4

675g/1½lb butternut squash, peeled and cut into chunks
1 onion, finely chopped
15g/½oz butter
1 bay leaf (optional)
860ml/1½ pints chicken or vegetable stock
salt and freshly ground black pepper
½ tablespoon chopped fresh thyme
4 tablespoons double cream (optional)

To serve
crusty white bread

1. Put the squash and onion into a large heavy saucepan with the butter. Cook gently for 10 minutes or until the vegetables begin to soften. Add the bay leaf, stock and a little salt and pepper.
2. Bring to the boil, then simmer as slowly as possible for 25 minutes or until the squash is soft.
3. Carefully liquidise the soup in a food processor or blender. Return to the rinsed-out saucepan. Stir in the thyme and cream and check the consistency. If the soup is too thin, reduce by rapidly boiling; if it is too thick, add extra stock or water.
4. Season to taste with salt and pepper. Serve with crusty white bread.

CAULIFLOWER CHEESE SOUP

If you ever have any leftover cauliflower cheese it can be whizzed up and made into a delicious soup. In fact, we like it so much we decided to write this recipe. It can be made in advance and then frozen or reheated as required.

Preparation time: 15 minutes
Cooking time: 10 minutes
Serves 4–6

1 tablespoon oil
1 onion, chopped
570ml/1 pint white stock
450g/1lb cauliflower, broken into
   florets and non-woody stems
   thinly sliced
200g/7oz strong Cheddar cheese,
   grated

85ml/3fl.oz double cream or
   crème fraîche
salt and pepper

To serve
croûtons

1. Heat the oil in a heavy-based saucepan, add the onion and sweat until transparent. Add the stock and cauliflower and cook until tender. Remove from the heat and stir in the Cheddar cheese.
2. Add the crème fraîche or cream and liquidise in a food processor or blender until very smooth.
3. Pour into a clean saucepan and reheat gently, but do not boil. Season with salt and pepper if necessary. Pour into warmed bowls and garnish with the croûtons.

PARSNIP AND CHICKPEA SOUP

This is a wonderfully rich creamy soup that is ideal for a winter evening. It makes plenty of soup for 6–8 people and can be prepared in advance and then frozen or reheated as required. Bacon can be salty so be careful not to over-season before adding the garnish.

Preparation time: 10 minutes
Cooking time: 25 minutes
Serves 6–8

1 tablespoon oil
1 medium onion, roughly chopped
285g/10oz parsnips, peeled and
  chopped
1.14 l/2 pints chicken or
  vegetable stock
1 × 400g/14oz can chickpeas,
  rinced and drained

2 tablespoons crème fraîche
salt and freshly ground black
  pepper

To serve
2 rashers bacon, cooked until
  crisp and cut into small pieces

1. Heat the oil in a large saucepan, add the onions and cook slowly until soft but not coloured.
2. Add the parsnips and stock. Bring to the boil and simmer until the parsnips are soft. Add the chickpeas.
3. Remove from the heat and allow to cool slightly. Add 1 tablespoon of the crème fraîche and liquidise in a blender or food processor. Add more stock or water to obtain your desired consistency, and season to taste with salt and pepper.
4. Reheat the soup and check the seasoning. Pour into warmed bowls and garnish each with a teaspoon of crème fraîche and a sprinkling of bacon.

TUSCAN WHITE BEAN SOUP

This delicious warming soup is ideal for a cold winter evening. Pushing the soup through a sieve is pretty time-consuming, but it does mean that you get a smooth texture. It can be made in advance and frozen or reheated as required. Both butter beans and cannellini beans are readily available in most supermarkets.

Preparation time: 25 minutes
Cooking time: 20 minutes
Serves 6

30g/1oz butter
1 large onion, finely chopped
2 sticks celery, finely chopped
2 cloves garlic, crushed
2 × 400g/14oz cans cooked
  butter beans, rinced and
  drained
2 × 400g/14oz cans cooked
  cannellini beans, rinced and
  drained

860ml/1½ pints good white
  chicken stock
salt and freshly ground white
  pepper
freshly grated nutmeg
2 tablespoons crème fraîche

To serve
chilli oil

1. Melt the butter in a large heavy-based saucepan. Add the onion and celery and sweat over a very low heat until soft but not coloured. Add the garlic and continue to cook for a further minute, ensuring that the vegetables take on no colour.

2. Add the butter beans and cannellini beans to the pan with the stock. Bring to the boil and simmer for 5 minutes. Remove from the heat and liquidise well in a food processor or blender.

3. Push the soup through a fine sieve and return to the rinsed-out pan. Add a little more stock or some milk if the soup is too thick. Stir in the crème fraîche, season to taste with the salt, ground white pepper and freshly grated nutmeg. Reheat gently.

4. Pour into warmed bowls and drizzle over a little chilli oil.

FENNEL AND CELERIAC SOUP

The bold flavours of the celeriac and fennel combine well in this simple winter soup, which is perfect drunk from mugs around the bonfire. The celeriac discolours quickly, so should not be peeled until required. However, the soup can be made in advance and then frozen and reheated as required.

Preparation time: 15 minutes
Cooking time: 35 minutes
Serves 4

30g/1oz butter
2 bulbs fennel, diced
225g/8oz celeriac, peeled and diced
1 onion, finely chopped
1 l/1¾ pints chicken stock
salt and freshly ground black pepper

To garnish
1 tablespoon finely chopped fresh parsley

1. Melt the butter in a saucepan. Add the fennel, celeriac and onion, then cover with a tight-fitting lid and sweat for 15–20 minutes or until the vegetables are just soft.

31

2. Add the chicken stock, salt and pepper and bring to the boil, then simmer for 15 minutes. Remove from the heat and allow to cool slightly.
3. Liquidise the soup in a food processor or blender until smooth and return to the rinsed-out saucepan. Adjust the seasoning and reheat gently. Serve garnished with fresh parsley.

HOT AND SOUR SOUP

This soup is quite simple to make and yet has a rather exotic Eastern flavour. It is made using raw, shell-on prawns so that the shells can be used to improve the stock. When you have peeled the prawns, the little black vein that runs down the back of each one remove with a sharp knife.

Preparation time: 20 minutes
Cooking time: 20 minutes
Serves 4

85g/3oz raw, shell-on prawns
425ml/¾ pint chicken stock
1 strip lime zest
2.5cm/1in piece lemon grass or 1
   strip lemon zest
½ red chilli, deseeded and thinly
   sliced
1 teaspoon light soy sauce
½ teaspoon finely chopped red
   chilli
pinch soft light-brown sugar

1 teaspoon freshly squeezed lime
   or lemon juice
55g/2oz button mushrooms, very
   thinly sliced
1 spring onion, thinly sliced
1 teaspoon coarsely chopped
   coriander

To serve
prawn crackers

1. Peel and devein the prawns reserving the shells. Put the shells into a pan with the stock, lime zest, lemon grass or lemon zest and sliced chilli. Bring to the boil, cover and simmer for 15 minutes.
2. Strain the stock into a clean pan. Add the soy sauce, chopped chilli, sugar and lime juice. Bring to the boil, then add the prawns, mushrooms and spring onion and simmer for 3 minutes. Stir in the coriander and serve, handing out the prawn crackers separately.

POTATO AND GARLIC SOUP

This is an unusual-sounding soup but the flavour of the garlic changes enormously once it is cooked – it stops being pungent and becomes mellow and sweet. This soup can be made in advance and then frozen or reheated as required.

Preparation time: 10 minutes
Cooking time: 20 minutes
Serves 4–6

3 tablespoons olive oil
8 cloves garlic, unpeeled
1 onion, chopped
450g/1lb potatoes, peeled and
   sliced
generous pinch ground saffron

salt and freshly ground black
   pepper
1.6 l/2½ pints chicken or
   vegetable stock
1 tablespoon chopped parsley

1. Preheat the oven to 200°C/400°F/gas mark 6.
2. Put the garlic into a small roasting tin, drizzle with 1 tablespoon of oil and bake for 10 minutes or until soft. Tip into a small bowl, add the remaining oil and leave to infuse for 10 minutes.

3. Strain the olive oil through a fine sieve and reserve. Peel the garlic cloves.
4. Heat the infused olive oil in a heavy-bottomed pan and cook the onion until soft but not coloured.
5. Add the potatoes, garlic, saffron, salt and pepper and stock. Simmer until the potatoes are soft.
6. Liquidise the soup in a food processor or blender and push through a sieve into the rinsed-out saucepan.
7. Season to taste and add water if the soup is too thick. Stir in the chopped parsley and reheat carefully.

BROCCOLI AND STILTON SOUP

This soup is a great comfort food for autumn and winter. Although it is available in cartons, the homemade variety is far superior in taste and texture. Served with crusty white bread it is ideal for the family, but it can also be served garnished with croûtons at supper parties. The soup is very quick and easy to make and can be prepared in advance and then frozen or reheated as required. Take care not to boil it once the cheese has been added, as this may cause the soup to curdle.

Preparation time: 15 minutes
Cooking time: 15 minutes
Serves 3–4

1 tablespoon oil
1 onion, chopped
450ml/¾ pint white stock
450g/1lb broccoli, broken into
  florets and non-woody stems
  thinly sliced

6 tablespoons crème fraîche
170g/6oz Stilton cheese, crumbled
salt and pepper

1. Heat the oil in a heavy-based saucepan, add the onion and sweat until transparent. Add the stock and broccoli and cook until tender. Remove from the heat.
2. Add the crème fraîche and Stilton and liquidise in a food processor or blender until very smooth.
3. Strain the soup into a clean saucepan and reheat gently, but do not boil. Season with salt and pepper if necessary.

TOMATO AND CARROT SOUP

Tomato and carrot soup is an excellent combination, as the sweetness of the carrots enhances the flavour of the tomatoes. This soup can be made in advance and then reheated or frozen as required, but the crème fraîche should be added only at the last minute.

Preparation time: 10 minutes
Cooking time: 20 minutes
Serves 4

30g/1oz butter
1 onion, chopped
4 carrots, peeled and sliced
6 tomatoes, roughly chopped

720ml/1¼ pints chicken stock
salt and freshly ground black pepper
2 tablespoons crème fraîche

1. Melt the butter in a large, heavy-based saucepan. Add the onions and carrots and cover the pan with a tight-fitting lid. Allow the vegetables to sweat until soft, approximately 10–15 minutes.
2. Add the chopped tomatoes and stock, bring to the boil and simmer for 5 minutes. Season to taste, then allow to cool slightly.
3. Liquidise in a food processor or blender and pass through a sieve into the rinsed-out pan. Reheat and stir through the crème fraîche. Serve immediately with crusty white bread.

BEAN AND PASTA SOUP

This soup is really a main-course dish – serve it simply with crusty white bread and a green salad. If you make it in advance, use less macaroni – it will continue to expand even once the soup has been cooked.

Preparation time: 10 minutes
Cooking time: 35 minutes
Serves 4–6

2 tablespoons olive oil
1 small red onion, chopped
2 stalks celery, diced into 1cm/
½in pieces
1 carrot, chopped into 1cm/½in
pieces
1 clove garlic, crushed
1 × 400g/14oz can chopped
plum tomatoes
1 courgette, cut into 1cm/½in
slices

1 l/1¾ pints chicken stock
85g/3oz small macaroni
1 × 400g/14oz can cannellini
beans, drained and rinsed
salt and freshly ground black
pepper

To serve
85g/3oz Parmesan cheese,
grated

1. Heat the oil in a pan and add the onion, celery and carrot. Cook gently until softened, approximately 10 minutes. Add the garlic and cook for 30 seconds.

2. Add the tomatoes, courgette and stock and bring to the boil, stirring constantly. Season with salt and pepper, then reduce the heat and simmer for 10 minutes.

3. Add the pasta and continue to simmer; when the pasta is cooked, add the beans and simmer for a further 3–4 minutes.

4. Season to taste and serve topped with the grated Parmesan.

SALADS

SMOKED MACKEREL AND NEW POTATO SALAD

This simple mackerel salad is perfect served as a first course for a dinner party or as a light summer lunch. It takes no time at all to prepare and can be made using leftover cooked new potatoes.

Preparation time: 8 minutes
Cooking time: 15 minutes
Serves 4

4 smoked mackerel fillets
3 tablespoons oil
1 tablespoon white wine vinegar
½ tablespoon grainy mustard
225g/8oz cooked new potatoes, sliced

1 bunch spring onions, sliced
1 bag mixed salad leaves
salt and freshly ground black pepper

1. Break the mackerel fillets into even-sized pieces.
2. Mix together the oil, white wine vinegar and grainy mustard.
3. Carefully mix together the mackerel, potatoes and spring onions, ensuring that the mackerel does not break up too much.
4. Divide the salad leaves between 4 serving plates. Gently spoon on the mackerel salad and drizzle with the mustard dressing.

WINTER SALAD WITH QUAIL'S EGGS AND PANCETTA

This salad is fiddly and expensive but, I think, well worth the effort for a dinner party. For family cooking, use hen's eggs (4, cut into quarters) and ready-made croûtons. Quail's eggs can be difficult to peel – roll them on a board until the shell is lightly cracked all over, then peel carefully; dipping them into cold water as necessary will speed up the process.

Preparation time: 25 minutes
Cooking time: 20 minutes
Serves 4

For the salad
16–20 *quail's eggs*
½ *ciabatta loaf, cut into 1cm/½in cubes*
3 *tablespoons olive oil*
1 × 130g/4½oz *packet ready-chopped pancetta*
1 *bag mixed salad leaves, such as rocket, radicchio and frisée*

For the dressing
3 *tablespoons extra virgin olive oil*
1 *tablespoon balsamic vinegar*
½ *teaspoon caster sugar*
¼ *teaspoon grainy mustard*

1. Cook the quail's eggs in simmering salted water for 3–4 minutes. Drain and rinse under cold running water. When cool, peel and cut in half.
2. Place the ciabatta cubes in one layer on a baking sheet and drizzle with the oil. Bake at 200°C/400°F/gas mark 6 for 5–10 minutes or until browned and crisp.
3. Meanwhile, fry the pancetta in a heavy pan until browned and crisp.
4. Make the dressing by whisking all the ingredients together.
5. Toss the salad leaves in the dressing and serve scattered with the pancetta, ciabatta croûtons and halved quail's eggs.

HONEYED GOAT'S CHEESE SALAD

This quick and simple first course is sophisticated enough for a dinner party but is so easy to make that it is suitable for family cooking. It is quite a robust dish, so there is no need to worry about it looking quite 'rustic'. It can be prepared ahead up to the end of stage 3 and then assembled at the last moment. The honey takes away the harsh edge that is sometimes associated with goat's cheese.

Preparation time: 10 minutes
Cooking time: 10 minutes
Serves 4

2 tablespoons oil	4 teaspoons runny honey
170g/6oz bacon lardons	2 tomatoes, peeled, deseeded and
4 tablespoons balsamic vinegar	diced
4 individual crottin	large handful mixed salad leaves

1. Heat 1 tablespoon of the oil in a heavy-based frying pan. Cook the lardons so that they are golden brown. Add the balsamic vinegar and the rest of the oil to the pan and deglaze. Leave in the pan but off the heat.
2. Cut the crottin horizontally in half, place on a baking sheet and drizzle the honey over the cut sides. Preheat the grill.
3. Wash and dry the salad leaves and break into bite-size pieces.
4. Grill the crottins cut-side up until golden brown and beginning to bubble.
5. Reheat the dressing and lardons. Add the tomatoes, pour the mixture over the salad leaves and toss together gently.
6. Arrange the salad on 4 plates with the crottin on top. Serve with crusty bread.

LENTIL, GREEN BEAN AND FETA SALAD

Puy lentils have a particularly delicious, nutty flavour that combines beautifully with the acidity of the feta cheese. All the ingredients can be prepared in advance but don't mix them together until you are ready to serve.

Preparation time: 5–10 minutes
Cooking time: 25 minutes
Serves 4

170g/6oz puy lentils
225g/8oz green beans, topped
 and tailed
1 punnet cherry tomatoes
3 tablespoons extra virgin olive oil
1 tablespoon balsamic vinegar

2 tablespoons finely chopped
 mint
1 bag mixed salad leaves
1 × 200g/7oz feta cheese,
 crumbled
salt and freshly ground black
 pepper

1. Place the lentils into a large pan of salted boiling water and cook for 15–20 minutes until just tender. Drain.
2. Blanch the green beans in boiling water for 1 minute and refresh in a bowl of cold water. Drain well.
3. Cut the cherry tomatoes in half.
4. To make the dressing, mix together the olive oil and balsamic vinegar, and salt and freshly ground black pepper to taste. Stir the mint into the dressing.
5. Mix together the lentils, beans, tomatoes and salad leaves. Add the dressing and mix lightly. Season to taste.
6. Pile on to a serving dish and scatter the crumbled feta cheese over the top.

CHICKEN LIVER SALAD TIÈDE

This delicious salad is perfect served as either a light lunch or a first course. It is also an economical dish to make, as chicken livers are relatively inexpensive. It is important that the livers are not overcooked and also that they are well cleaned, otherwise they will have a bitter taste.

Preparation time: 20 minutes
Cooking time: 5 minutes
Serves 2–4

30g/1oz butter
110g/4oz chicken livers, cleaned
¼ head frisée lettuce, washed and
 picked into bite-size pieces
2 hard-boiled eggs, each cut into
 6 pieces

Parmesan cheese shavings

For the croûtons
2 slices white bread, cubed
1 tablespoon olive oil

For the dressing
6 *tablespoons olive oil*
2 *tablespoons white wine vinegar*

1 *tablespoon grainy mustard*
salt and freshly ground black
  pepper

1. Preheat the oven to 150°C/300°F/gas mark 2.
2. Make the croûtons: put the bread cubes on to a baking sheet, drizzle with the olive oil and season with salt and pepper. Bake in the oven until crisp and golden brown.
3. Make the dressing by mixing together all the ingredients.
4. Heat the butter in a pan until it foams, then add the livers and cook for about 2 minutes. Pour the dressing into the pan and stir quickly.
5. Put the frisée into a large bowl. Scatter the chicken livers in their dressing, the croûtons and eggs over the leaves. Garnish with the Parmesan shavings and serve immediately.

AVOCADO, POTATO AND BACON SALAD

This delicious salad improves if it has been prepared to the end of stage 2 in advance – the potatoes should absorb as much of the dressing as possible. The recipe calls for soft-boiled eggs – meaning that the yolk should be just set: to achieve this, cook the eggs in salted boiling water for 8 minutes. Vulnerable groups (i.e. the elderly, pregnant, sick and the very young) should use hard-boiled eggs or omit them completely.

Preparation time: 15 minutes
Cooking time: 20 minutes
Serves 4

5 *tablespoons olive oil*
170g/6oz *bacon lardons*
3 *tablespoons balsamic vinegar*
salt and freshly ground black
  pepper
340g/12oz *new potatoes, cut*
  horizontally in half

2 *avocado pears*
1 *bag mixed salad leaves*

To serve
4 *soft-boiled eggs, cut in half, or*
  4 *poached eggs*
1 *tablespoon chopped chives*

1. Heat a tablespoon of the oil in a heavy-based frying pan, add the bacon and cook until golden brown. Add the rest of the oil and the balsamic vinegar, season with black pepper and set aside.

2. Boil the new potatoes in salted water until cooked, then drain and return to the pan. Reheat the dressing and bacon and immediately pour the mixture over the potatoes. Toss together gently, put the lid on the pan and leave to sit and absorb the dressing while you prepare the other ingredients.
3. Peel the avocado and cut into slices or chunks. Mix together the salad leaves and the avocado and then divide between 4 plates. Pile the potato and bacon on to the centre of each bed of salad leaves.
4. Finally, place the soft-boiled or poached eggs on the very top of each pile and garnish with chopped chives.

MACKEREL WITH FENNEL AND TOMATO SALSA

When buying mackerel it is essential that they are absolutely fresh. Your fishmonger will gut and clean them for you if you ask, but even then you must ensure that they have been well cleaned. Serve with new potatoes and a green salad.

Preparation time: 20 minutes
Cooking time: 15 minutes
Serves 4

4 gutted and cleaned mackerel
7 tablespoons olive oil
salt and freshly ground black
  pepper
1 bulb fennel, very finely chopped
½ red onion, very finely chopped
juice of 2 lemons

2 tomatoes, finely chopped and
  deseeded
3 tablespoons coriander, freshly
  chopped

To garnish
small bunch watercress

1. Preheat the oven to 175°C/375°F/gas mark 5.
2. Place each mackerel on a piece of tinfoil lined with an oiled sheet of greaseproof paper (this helps to keep the fish beautifully moist). Pour 4 tablespoons of olive oil over the fish and season with black pepper and a pinch of salt. Wrap up the fish, scrunching the foil to seal.
3. Place on a baking sheet and bake in the preheated oven for 15–20 minutes depending on the size of the fish.
4. Mix together the remaining oil, the fennel, onion, tomato, lemon juice and coriander. Season with salt and pepper and set aside to allow the flavours to infuse.
5. Remove each fish from the tinfoil parcels and serve, with the juices and a generous spoonful of the salsa, garnished with watercress.

TROUT IN PROSCIUTTO WITH FENNEL SALAD

This is a simple fish dish to prepare but is sophisticated enough to serve for a dinner party. The fish can be wrapped several hours in advance and the flavour of the salad will improve considerably if allowed to stand for a couple of hours.

Preparation time: 20 minutes
Cooking time: 10 minutes
Serves 4

4 trout fillets, skinned and pinboned
8 slices prosciutto
1 tablespoon olive oil

For the salad
1 large bulb fennel, very thinly
  sliced

juice of 1 lemon
75 ml/2½fl oz good-quality extra
  virgin olive oil
55g/2oz good-quality black olives,
  pitted
salt and freshly ground black
  pepper

1. Lay 2 slices of prosciutto on a board so that they overlap slightly. Place 1 trout fillet on the prosciutto and season well with pepper.
2. Fold the prosciutto over the trout fillet so that it is completely enclosed.
3. Repeat steps 1 and 2 for the remaining 3 fillets.
4. Chill in the refrigerator for 15 minutes.
5. Meanwhile, prepare the salad. Place the fennel in a bowl. Mix together

the lemon juice and olive oil and pour over the fennel. Add the olives and season with salt and pepper.

6. Heat the oil in a large heavy frying pan and fry the fillets, seam-side up, until the prosciutto is crisp and the fish is cooked.

7. Serve immediately with the fennel salad.

GRILLED GOAT'S CHEESE WITH WARM LENTIL SALAD

This makes for an elegant first course for a dinner party. The lentil salad can be completely prepared in advance and then reheated in the microwave or in a saucepan while the crottin are under the grill.

Preparation time: 20 minutes
Cooking time: 20 minutes
Serves 4

170g/6oz puy lentils
few sprigs thyme
2 bay leaves
1 tablespoon oil
1 red onion, sliced
2 tablespoons balsamic vinegar
1 tablespoon soft dark-brown sugar
4 small individual goat's cheeses
  (crottin)

110g/4oz chopped bacon, cooked
  until crisp
55g/2oz walnuts, roughly
  chopped (optional)
handful sage leaves, chopped
handful flat-leaf parsley, chopped
extra virgin olive oil

1. Cook the lentils in a large saucepan of boiling water with the thyme and bay leaves – this should take about 15–20 minutes.

2. In another pan, heat the oil. Add the red onions and sweat until soft, then add the balsamic vinegar and sugar and allow the onions to caramelise.

3. Preheat the grill. Grill the crottin until the tops are brown and bubbling.

4. Drain the lentils, add the bacon, walnuts, chopped herbs, onion and olive oil. Mix together well and season to taste with salt and pepper.

5. Serve each crottin on a bed of the warm salad.

BLT SALAD

Bacon, lettuce and tomato is one of the most satisfying sandwich combinations, with the salty and powerful flavour of the bacon combining with the sweetness of the tomatoes. Here the simple ingredients are made into a salad, which can be prepared in advance and combined at the last minute or prepared and served within about 30 minutes. Ready-made croûtons can also be used to save time. This salad can be served as a first course or as a snack – it makes a particularly good brunch dish.

Preparation and cooking time: 15 minutes
Serves 4

8 rashers rindless smoked streaky
   bacon
110g/4oz cherry tomatoes
oil for frying
½ focaccia or ciabatta loaf, cut
   into 1.5cm/1in chunks (reserve
   the remainder of the loaf)
4 plum or salad tomatoes

4 tablespoons mayonnaise
2 tablespoons water
1 tablespoon coarse grainy
   mustard
1 × 225g/8oz pack of mixed
   continental salad leaves
salt and freshly ground black
   pepper

1. Preheat the oven to 200°C/400°F/gas mark 6.
2. Using the back of a knife, stretch out the bacon rashers on a chopping board. Place on a baking sheet with the cherry tomatoes and bake in the oven until the rashers are crisp and brown, but remove the cherry tomatoes when they soften and begin to colour (after about 5–6 minutes).
3. Heat the frying oil in a heavy-based pan. The oil should be at least 1cm/½in deep, and is hot enough to start frying in when a piece of bread sizzles and browns in it in about 20 seconds. Fry the cubes of bread a handful at a time until evenly browned. Stir with a slotted metal spoon, then drain on absorbent paper and sprinkle with a little salt. Keep warm.
4. Slice the plum tomatoes. Whisk together the mayonnaise, water and mustard and season to taste with salt and pepper.
5. Break the bacon rashers into pieces, then toss together with the salad, dressing, tomatoes, cherry tomatoes and salt and pepper. Pile on to plates and garnish with the croûtons. Serve with the remaining bread.

WARM ROCKET AND BROAD BEAN SALAD

This salad can be served as a first course or as an accompaniment to a main course. It calls for frozen broad beans but when fresh ones are in season buy considerably more (about 900g/2lb) pod, then cook and remove the outer shells – children often dislike broad beans, but seem to enjoy them more when they are podded and not so easily identifiable.

Preparation time: 10 minutes
Cooking time: 5 minutes
Serves 4

1 tablespoon extra virgin olive oil
1 × 70g/2½oz packet Parma ham, cut into strips
225g/8oz frozen young broad beans
1 tablespoon wholegrain mustard

2 tablespoons cider vinegar
salt and freshly ground black pepper
170g/6oz rocket, washed and picked over

1. Heat the oil in a heavy frying pan and cook the Parma ham until crisp.
2. Meanwhile, cook the broad beans in boiling salted water. Drain well and add to the Parma ham.
3. Stir in the mustard and vinegar and season to taste with salt and pepper.
4. Add the rocket and stir until just wilted.
5. Serve immediately.

SAVOURY DISHES

DUCK AND SHIITAKE MUSHROOM SPRING ROLLS

These spring rolls are made using ready-cooked barbecued duck or chicken now widely available in many supermarkets. The spring-roll wrappers are generally available only at specialist food shops, but they are often sold frozen so you can buy several packets at once – they will keep for up to 3 months. We have found that a fairly wet flour-and-water paste makes an effective glue to hold the wrappers in place. The spring rolls can be completely prepared in advance and then deep-fried when required.

Preparation time: 25 minutes
Cooking time: 5 minutes
Serves 4

1 small barbecued duck or
   chicken
170g/6oz shiitake mushrooms,
   finely sliced
15g/½oz butter
8 large spinach leaves
16 spring-roll wrappers
55g/2oz bean sprouts
salt and freshly ground black
   pepper

a little flour-and-water paste
oil for deep frying

To serve
hoisin sauce or chilli dipping
   sauce

To garnish
fresh coriander

1. Take the duck off the bone and shred the meat finely. Set aside.
2. Fry the mushrooms slowly in the butter until tender and quite dry. The mushrooms will initially give off liquid – continue to fry until this has all evaporated. Drain on kitchen paper.

47

3. Blanch the spinach leaves in boiling salted water, refresh under running cold water and drain well.

4. Arrange the spring-roll wrappers on a board. Cover each one with a piece of spinach. Divide the shredded duck, mushrooms and bean sprouts between the spring rolls. Season lightly with salt and pepper. Put the filling in the centre of each wrapper and fold 2 opposite corners on top of it. Then roll up from one of the exposed corners to the other to form rolls. Seal lightly with the flour-and-water paste.

5. Heat the oil in a deep-fat fryer until a crumb will sizzle vigorously in it, and add the spring rolls. Fry until golden brown, then drain well on absorbent paper.

6. Sprinkle with salt and serve with the hoisin or chilli dipping sauce, garnished with the fresh coriander.

CRAB AND PRAWN ROLLS

These spring rolls are unusual, easy to make and can be prepared in advance and then frozen (providing you don't use frozen prawns) as required. They can be served as a canapé or as a first course. Spring-roll wrappers are available from most Asian specialist shops; they freeze well so buy several packets at a time.

Preparation time: 30 minutes
Cooking time: 2 minutes
Makes 12–15

15g/½oz butter
3 spring onions, finely sliced
1 small red chilli, chopped finely
2 teaspoons pickled ginger, finely chopped
2 170g/6oz cans crab meat, drained
110g/4oz cooked prawns
zest of 1 lime

salt and freshly ground black pepper
1 packet spring-roll wrappers
lightly beaten egg white
oil for frying

To serve
mild chilli dipping sauce

1. In a small frying pan, heat the butter and fry the spring onions until soft.

2. Mix together the chilli, ginger, crab, prawns and lime zest and season with salt and pepper. Stir in the spring onions.

3. Arrange the spring-roll wrappers on a board. Divide the filling between the spring-roll wrappers. Put the filling in the centre of each wrapper and fold 2 opposite corners on top of it. Then roll up from one of the exposed corners to form rolls. Brush the rolls with the beaten egg white.
4. Heat the oil in a deep-fat fryer or large heavy-based pan until a crumb will sizzle vigorously in it and add the spring rolls. Fry until golden brown, then drain well on absorbent kitchen paper.
5. Sprinkle lightly with salt and serve immediately with a dipping sauce.

SIMPLE NORI SUSHI ROLLS

The ingredients for making sushi are now readily available in supermarkets. Sushi is traditionally filled with a variety of fillings, such as avocado pear, peeled cucumber, smoked salmon, raw fish, cooked prawns, squid and scallops and strips of sweet omelette. This recipe simply uses smoked salmon, avocado and cucumber. A sushi mat helps to make rolling the sushi easy but is not necessary.

Preparation time: 30 minutes
Makes: 60

225g/8oz sushi rice
450ml/16fl oz water
1 piece kombu seaweed
5 tablespoons rice wine vinegar
1 tablespoon caster sugar
2 teaspoons salt
1 packet nori seaweed, ready
  roasted
½ cucumber, peeled and cut into
  long pencil lengths

110g/4oz smoked salmon, cut
  into strips
1 avocado pear, peeled and cut
  into strips

To serve
3 tablespoons soy sauce
1 red chilli, finely chopped
wasabi paste

1. Rinse the rice under running cold water. Put the rice into a saucepan with the water and kombu, bring to the boil, cover and simmer for 12 minutes. Remove the kombu and add the vinegar, sugar and salt. Mix and leave to cool.
2. Lay a sushi mat or thick napkin on a work surface. Cover with a piece of nori seaweed. Spoon a layer of rice over two-thirds of each sheet, up to the edges.

3. Arrange a couple of cucumber and avocado strips and a piece of smoked salmon on the rice. Roll up firmly as for a Swiss roll, using the sushi mat or napkin to help you. Roll the remaining sushi. Leave to stand for 15 minutes.
4. Trim the edges of the seaweed and cut each roll crosswise into 5–6 even slices.
5. Mix the soy and chilli together.
6. Serve with the soy and chilli as a dipping sauce and hand the wasabi separately (it is very strong).

BEETROOT AND GOAT'S CHEESE TARTS

These delicious little tarts are very simple to make and yet they look and taste very sophisticated. They are perfect as a first course for a spring lunch. Alternatively they can be served as a main course with a tomato salad and a few hot new potatoes. Tiny versions can also be made and served as a canapé.

Preparation time: 10 minutes
Cooking time: 20 minutes
Serves 6

225g/8oz packet puff pastry
1 packet ready-cooked beetroot
2 × 200g/7oz rolled goat's
cheese with skin
2 tablespoons olive oil
salt and pepper

For the dressing
3 tablespoons ready-made basil
pesto
1 tablespoon balsamic vinegar
3 tablespoons olive oil

To garnish
rocket leaves

1. Preheat the oven to 200°C/400°F/gas mark 6.
2. Roll out the puff pastry to 2.5mm/⅛in thick and cut out 7.5cm/3in-diameter rounds and place on a baking sheet.
3. Slice the beetroot and the goat's cheese into 5mm/¼in slices and arrange on the top of the pastry, starting with a layer of beetroot followed by a layer of goat's cheese. Chill in the refridgerator for 15 minutes.
4. Drizzle the olive oil over the top of the tarts and sprinkle with salt and pepper. Bake in the preheated oven for about 20 minutes or until golden brown.
5. Mix together the dressing ingredients.
6. Put each tart on a plate and serve, garnished with the rocket leaves and a drizzle of the pesto dressing.

DUCK EGGS BENEDICT WITH PARMA HAM

This recipe calls for duck eggs, which are delicious, but hen eggs can be used instead should you prefer. The best way to poach an egg is to use a large sauté pan. Crack the egg into a cup and tip it very gently into near-boiling salted water – get the cup as close to the water as possible. Reduce the heat, and as the egg rises to the surface it will begin to set. It may be necessary to trim raggedy pieces of white with a pair of kitchen scissors. Using a slotted spoon, lift the egg out of the pan, then rest the spoon on kitchen paper to drain.

Preparation time: 10 minutes
Cooking time: 5 minutes

4 English muffins, split
horizontally in half and toasted
2 slices Parma ham, cut in half
4 fresh duck eggs
1 small jar ready-to-use

hollandaise sauce
chopped fresh parsley
squeeze of lemon juice
salt and freshly ground black
pepper

1. Preheat the grill and bring a large shallow pan of water to the boil.
2. Meanwhile, crack the eggs and poach for 2–3 minutes or until set.
3. Heat the hollandaise sauce according to the instructions and mix half of the sauce with the chopped parsley. Spread over the toasted muffins.
4. Put a piece of Parma ham on to each muffin half, trim it to size and top with a poached egg.
5. Spoon the remaining sauce over the eggs and grill for 30 seconds or until bubbling and lightly browned. Serve immediately.

PESTO PIZZAS

This recipe is a real cheat as it calls for a commercially prepared pizza mix. Making your own dough will invariably give much better results, but a packet mixture produces far nicer pizzas than buying and reheating ready-made bases.

Preparation time: 25 minutes
Cooking time: 25 minutes
Makes 2 × 22cm/9in or 4 × 11cm/4½in pizzas

1 × 280g/9½oz packet pizza mix
water
5 tablespoons basil pesto
170g/6oz sunblushed tomatoes in oil, drained and chopped (reserve the oil)
110g/4oz Gorgonzola cheese, sliced
110g/4oz mozzarella cheese, sliced
5 slices Parma ham, cut into strips
freshly ground black pepper
1 large bag rocket
balsamic vinegar
olive oil

1. Preheat the oven to 220°C/425°F/gas mark 7.
2. Make up the pizza base following the instructions on the packet, but adding the pesto in place of 5 tablespoons of the water called for.
3. Divide the dough into 2 or 4. Roll out into circles, drizzle with half the tomato oil and allow to rise in a warm place for 20 minutes.
4. Cook the bases in the oven for 15–20 minutes, until cooked through.
5. As soon as the bases are cooked, layer the tomatoes and cheeses over the top and cover loosely with the ham. Drizzle some of the reserved tomato oil over the pizzas and season with a little freshly ground black pepper. Return to the oven for 5–7 minutes.

6. Meanwhile dress the rocket salad with the oil and vinegar.
7. Remove the pizzas from the oven and place a large handful of the rocket salad on the top of each one. Serve immediately.

CHERRY TOMATO TATIN

This delicious tomato tatin can be prepared in advance and then baked just before you are ready to serve. Allow the tatin to cool slightly before serving, as the baked tomatoes are very hot.

Preparation time: 10 minutes
Cooking time: 30 minutes
Serves 4–6

2 tablespoons oil
700g/1lb 9oz cherry tomatoes,
stalks removed
2 tablespoons fresh thyme,
chopped

salt and freshly ground black
pepper
2 teaspoons caster sugar
1 × 225g/8oz packet puff pastry
150ml/¼pint balsamic vinegar

1. Preheat the oven to 200°C/400°F/gas mark 6.
2. Pour the oil into a 25cm/10in metal-handled frying pan. Add the tomatoes, thyme, salt, pepper and sugar. Shake to ensure that the tomatoes are covered in the seasonings.
3. Roll out the pastry to a 25cm/10in circle the thickness of a 1p coin. Place the pastry over the top of the tomatoes in the pan. Place in the oven and bake for 20 minutes or until the pastry is golden brown.
4. Remove the frying pan from the oven. Place your hand lightly on the pastry and strain any liquid from the pan into a small saucepan.

5. Add the vinegar to the reserved juices, bring to the boil and then reduce to a syrupy consistency.
6. Meanwhile invert a large plate over the pastry and turn out the tatin (be very careful: any remaining hot juices will come out from under the pastry).
7. Drizzle the reduced balsamic vinegar and juices over the top of the tatin and serve immediately with a green salad.

RED ONION, FETA AND PINE NUT TART

This recipe involves use of a commercially prepared pre-baked pastry flan. Flans are now widely available in most supermarkets. If making your own pastry, a 170g/6oz flour quantity should be plenty. The tart can be served as a first course, or as a supper dish with baked potatoes and a green salad.

Preparation time: 20 minutes
Cooking time: 25–30 minutes
Serves 4

30g/1oz butter
1 large red onion, sliced
1 red pepper, seeded and sliced
2 eggs
75ml/2½fl oz double cream
110g/4oz feta cheese, crushed

2 teaspoons fresh thyme
salt and freshly ground black
  pepper
1 pre-baked 20cm/8in diameter
  shortcrust pastry case
30g/1oz pine nuts, toasted

1. Preheat the oven to 170°C/375°F/gas mark 3.
2. Melt the butter and add the onion, then cook slowly for 10 minutes. Add the pepper and cook for a further 10 minutes.
3. Mix the eggs, cream, feta cheese and thyme together and season lightly with salt and pepper (feta is quite salty).
4. Place the onions and peppers on the base of the flan and sprinkle the pine nuts over the top. Gently pour the egg and cheese mixture into the case.
5. Bake in the preheated oven for 25 minutes or until the filling has set.

CRAB AND ASPARAGUS TART

This recipe calls for half a can of crab or lobster bisque, as this will improve the flavour of the finished dish. If bisque is unavailable, use 150ml/¼ pint double cream in its place.

Preparation time: 12 minutes
Cooking time: 55 minutes
Serves 4–6

225g/8oz shortcrust pastry	1½ tablespoons fresh dill, finely
1 tablespoon oil	chopped
2 shallots, finely chopped	1 × 170g/6oz can crabmeat,
6–8 spears of asparagus	drained
2 eggs, beaten	salt and pepper
150ml/¼ pint crab or lobster bisque	1 tablespoon juice lemon

1. Preheat the oven to 200°C/400°F/gas mark 6. Roll out the shortcrust pastry to line a 20cm/8in flan ring. Allow to chill in the refridgerator for 30 minutes, then bake blind in the preheated oven.
2. Reduce the oven temperature to 190°C/375°F/gas mark 5.
3. Meanwhile, heat the oil in a heavy-based saucepan and sweat the shallots until soft but not coloured.
4. Prepare the asparagus: trim off the woody ends – if you bend the stems they tend to snap into two, leaving you with one end to discard (the root

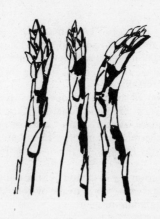

end) and one to keep. Trim the spears from the tip into 10cm/4in lengths and reserve. Cut the rest of the stems into slices, add to the onion mix and soften. Remove from the heat and allow to cool.

5. Very lightly blanch and refresh the reserved asparagus tips.

6. Beat together the eggs and add the bisque, the asparagus and onion mixture, dill, crabmeat, plenty of salt and pepper and the lemon juice. Pour the mixture into the pastry case and arrange the asparagus tips on the top. Bake in the preheated oven for 25–30 minutes, until just set and lightly brown.

OPEN ONION TARTS

These tarts can be served as a first course or supper dish. They can be prepared to the end of stage 5 in advance. Reheat the onion, pile atop of the pastry and place in the oven to reheat for 5 minutes.

Preparation time: 20 minutes
Cooking time: 25 minutes
Makes 4

2 tablespoons oil
675g/1½lb onions, very finely sliced
1 tablespoon fresh thyme, chopped
salt and freshly ground black pepper

1½ tablespoons soft dark-brown sugar
1 × 225g/8oz packet puff pastry
55g/2oz goat's cheese, crumbled
flour for rolling

1. Preheat the oven to 200°C/400°F/gas mark 6.

2. Put the oil, onions, thyme, salt and pepper and sugar in a large roasting pan. Stir to cover the onions in the seasonings, and bake in the oven for 15 minutes. Stir again and continue to cook, turning them regularly, until the onions are soft and caramelised.

3. Meanwhile, on a floured surface, roll out the pastry to the thickness of a 20p coin and cut into 4 × 15cm/6in squares. Mark a border around the outer edge of each square, and prick the centre of the squares all over with a fork. Chill in the refridgerator for 15 minutes.

4. Bake the pastry on the top shelf of the oven for 15–20 minutes or until brown and crisp.

5. Remove the pastry from the oven and fill the centre with the onions, sprinkle over the goat's cheese, return to the oven for 3 minutes or until the goat's cheese is just beginning to melt.

6. Serve immediately.

BACON AND CHEESE PUFFS

These puffs can be prepared in advance and then baked when
required. They make delicious snacks and can be eaten with a green
salad for an informal lunch. As an extra to this recipe put a couple of
slices of tomato between the bacon and cheese. The quantity of grainy
mustard used can be varied depending on taste; if preparing the puffs
for children, tomato sauce can be used instead of the mustard.

Preparation time: 10 minutes
Cooking time: 30 minutes
Serves 4

1 × 375g/13oz packet puff
   pastry
1 tablespoon grainy mustard
8 rashers bacon, cooked

110g/4oz strong hard cheese, such
   as Cheddar, grated
ground black pepper
1 egg, beaten

1. Preheat the oven to 200°C/400°F/gas mark 6.
2. Roll out pastry to the thickness of a 50p coin and cut out 4 × 13cm/5in
squares.

3. Spread a quarter of the mustard on each square, then lay 2 slices of bacon diagonally across each square. Sprinkle the grated cheese over the bacon and season with a little ground black pepper.

4. Fold up the other 2 corners of each square so that they meet in the middle along the length of the bacon, then lightly push this seam down into the centre of the square. Put the puffs on to a baking sheet and brush each one with beaten egg, then chill in the refrigerator for 20–30 minutes.

5. Bake in the preheated oven for 20 minutes, until the pastry is golden brown.

BLUE CHEESE AND LEEK TARTLETS

These tartlets can be prepared in advance and then frozen or reheated as required. They can be served as a first course, snack or supper dish, and can even be made in miniature and served as canapés. They seem to be popular with adults and children alike.

Preparation time: 30 minutes
Cooking time: 30 minutes
Serves 4

225g/8oz frozen puff pastry,
  defrosted
30g/1oz butter
2 medium leeks, outer leaves
  discarded, finely chopped and
  well washed
170g/6oz strong blue cheese,
  crumbled

45g/1½oz ham, sliced (optional)
1 tablespoon Dijon mustard
  (optional)
freshly ground black pepper
egg to glaze

To serve
green salad

1. Preheat the oven to 200°C/400°F/gas mark 6. Heat the butter in a heavy-based saucepan, then add the leeks and cook until soft, allowing any liquid to be driven off. Remove from the heat and allow to cool.

2. Roll out the pastry to the thickness of a 50p coin and cut into 4 × 12cm/ 4½in squares. Using a sharp knife, score diagonally across the corners of each square but don't cut through the pastry. Prick the centre of the pastry case all over. Place the squares on an ovenproof sheet and chill in the refrigerator for at least 15 minutes.

3. Add the ham, if using, and 110g/4oz of the cheese to the leeks. Season with black pepper.

4. Spread the mustard (if using) over the centre of each chilled pastry

square. Then pile on the leek and cheese mixture, making sure it reaches the edges and covers the mustard. Sprinkle the remaining cheese over the top.
5. Brush the scored corners of each square with beaten egg and return to the refridgerator for 15 minutes.
6. Bake in the preheated oven for 20 minutes or until the pastry is golden brown and cooked through.
7. Serve warm with a green salad.

CREAMY FISH FLAN WITH BURNT HOLLANDAISE

This is one of our favourite flans at Leith's School. We have incorporated some commercially prepared ingredients to make it quicker to prepare than it usually is. If the fish has been poached in milk, reserve the cooking liquor for the white sauce. The ready-made hollandaise used must be of a variety in a jar or carton rather than the packet version. Serve this dish with a green salad.

Preparation time: 20 minutes
Cooking time: 30 minutes
Serves 4

1 pre-baked 20cm/8in pastry case
1 small onion, finely chopped
30g/1oz butter
30g/1oz plain flour
1 bay leaf
290ml/½ pint milk
salt and freshly ground black pepper

1 egg, separated
225g/8oz white fish, cooked and flaked
1 tablespoon chopped fresh parsley
squeeze of lemon juice
1 × small jar ready-made hollandaise

1. Preheat the oven temperature to 180°C/350°F/gas mark 4.
2. Cook the onion in the butter in a saucepan until soft but not coloured. Add the flour and bay leaf. Cook, stirring, for 1 minute. Remove from the heat, stir in the milk, and bring slowly to the boil, stirring continuously. Taste and season as necessary with salt and pepper. Simmer for 2 minutes, remove the bay leaf and allow to cool for 5 minutes.
3. Beat the egg yolk into the sauce. Stir in the fish and parsley, and the lemon juice to taste. Whisk the egg white until stiff but not dry and fold

into the mixture. Pour into the pastry case. Bake in the centre of the preheated oven for about 25 minutes.

4. Preheat the grill 10 minutes before the flan is cooked.

5. Spoon the hollandaise over the flan. Put the flan under the hot grill until the top is nicely browned. Serve immediately.

LEMON AND ARTICHOKE TARTLETS

Although this recipe calls for ready-rolled pastry, we suggest re-rolling it with the addition of lemon zest, which gives a refreshingly delicious flavour to the finished dish. When rolling puff pastry do so with short sharp strokes – do not be tempted to roll it into a ball or you may roll away the layers.

Preparation time: 15 minutes
Cooking time: 15 minutes
Serves 4

1 × 375g/12oz packet ready-rolled puff pastry
flour for rolling
zest of 1 lemon, finely grated
salt and freshly ground black pepper
1 egg, beaten

55g/2oz crème fraîche
2 teaspoons lemon juice
1 × 400g/14oz can artichoke hearts, drained
2 tablespoons extra virgin lemon olive oil

1. Preheat the oven to 200°C/400°F/gas mark 6.
2. Lay the pastry on to a lightly floured work surface. Sprinkle the lemon zest over the pastry and season with salt and pepper. Fold the pastry in half and roll it out to the thickness of a 20p coin.
3. Using a saucer as a guide, cut out 4 circles about 10cm/4in in diameter. Lay them on to a floured baking sheet. Brush with the beaten egg and chill in the refridgerator for 10 minutes.
4. Meanwhile, mix the crème fraîche and the lemon juice together and season with salt and pepper.
5. Divide the mixture between the pastry circles and spread almost to the edges.
6. Cut the artichoke hearts in half and arrange, cut-side up, in a circle on top of the crème fraîche. Press down well. Season the tartlets with salt and pepper and drizzle oil over each one.
7. Bake on the top shelf of the oven for 15–20 minutes or until the pastry is risen and well browned. Serve hot or warm.

STEAKS ON CIABATTA WITH MUSTARD BUTTER

This recipe calls for ciabatta bread because it can absorb meat juices and butter without becoming immediately soggy. The steaks must be cooked at the last minute – if kept warm for any length of time they will begin to toughen.

Preparation time: 15 minutes
Cooking time: 5 minutes
Serves 4

1 ciabatta loaf, sliced horizontally
   in half
55g/2oz unsalted butter, softened
1½ tablespoons wholegrain
   mustard
1 tablespoon runny honey
1 tablespoon oil

4 × 140g/5oz sirloin steaks,
   trimmed
salt and freshly ground black
   pepper
1 bunch watercress, stalks
   removed, roughly chopped
1½ tablespoons water
1 tablespoon balsamic vinegar

1. Preheat the oven to 200°C/400°F/gas mark 6. Put the ciabatta into the oven to heat through.
2. Meanwhile, make the mustard butter. Put the butter, mustard and honey into a small bowl and beat together. Season with black pepper. Set aside.
3. Heat the oil in a frying pan. Season the steaks with salt and black pepper. Brown on both sides and reduce the heat. Cook for a further 2–3 minutes or until pink.
4. Remove the steaks from the pan and keep warm. Pour the water and vinegar into the pan and bring to the boil.
5. Spread the mustard butter on each piece of ciabatta and cut in half.
6. Divide the watercress between the four pieces of bread, pour the pan juices over the top and top each piece with a steak. Serve immediately.

CURRIED CHICKEN AND MANGO NAAN SANDWICH

This delicious sandwich is an ideal way of using up leftover cooked chicken or turkey. The sauce can be prepared in advance and then kept overnight in the refridgerator. The same recipe can be used, without the naan bread, as a main course for a buffet party.

Preparation time: 10 minutes
Cooking time: 15 minutes
Serves 4

285g/10oz cooked chicken
1 tablespoon medium curry paste,
  such as mild korma paste
3 tablespoons mango chutney,
  chopped
2 tablespoons Greek yoghurt
zest of 1 lime, finely grated
salt and freshly ground black pepper

1 small gem lettuce heart,
  shredded
½ bunch spring onions, finely
  sliced
55g/2oz coriander leaves, roughly
  chopped
2 plain naan bread

1. Preheat the oven to 200°C/400°F/gas mark 6.
2. Mix the curry paste, mango chutney and Greek yoghurt together in a small bowl. Add the lime zest and season with salt and black pepper. Stir in

the shredded lettuce, spring onions and coriander leaves and set aside.

3. Cut the naan bread in half and place on a baking sheet. Heat in the oven for 5 minutes or until puffed up.

4. Shred the chicken flesh and divide between the warm naan pockets along with the lettuce and onion mixture.

BALSAMIC GLAZED CHICKEN LIVERS ON CORIANDER TOAST

Chicken livers are available fresh or frozen from most good supermarkets. They have a wonderfully rich flavour but cost relatively little to buy. It is very important that they are well washed and picked over before they are cooked, as liver can have a bitter flavour. If brioche is unavailable, use slices of thick white bread – the brioche simply adds to the richness of the dish. If you do not like coriander use flat-leaf parsley in its place.

Preparation time: 10 minutes
Cooking time: 10 minutes
Serves 4

55g/2oz unsalted butter
½ bunch or 1 packet fresh
  coriander leaves, chopped
salt and freshly ground black
  pepper
1 teaspoon lemon juice
4 thick slices brioche
1 bunch spring onions, trimmed
  and very finely chopped

340g/12oz fresh chicken livers,
  washed and picked over
2 tablespoons water
2 tablespoons good-quality
  balsamic vinegar

To garnish
coriander leaves

1. Preheat the grill.

2. Soften 45g/1½oz of the butter in a small bowl; beat in the coriander leaves and season with salt, pepper and lemon juice.

3. Toast the brioche lightly on both sides, then spread the coriander butter on each slice and keep warm.

4. Melt the remaining butter in a frying pan and fry the spring onions for 1–2 minutes or until they begin to brown. Add the chicken livers and fry briskly for 2–3 minutes, until browned on the outside but still pink in the middle.

5. Pour the water and balsamic vinegar into the pan, bring to the boil and simmer for 1 minute. Season with salt and black pepper.

6. Spoon the chicken livers on to the hot coriander toast and pour the balsamic glaze over the top. Garnish with coriander leaves and serve immediately.

PARMESAN AND PEAR RAREBIT

This is simply a variation of Welsh rarebit – it can be served as a canapé if the toast is cut into small pieces, or as a snack or supper dish served with a green salad.

Preparation time: 10 minutes
Cooking time: 10 minutes
Serves 4

85g/3oz Cheddar cheese, freshly grated
85g/3oz Parmesan cheese, freshly grated
1 Conference pear, skin on, grated

1 teaspoon Dijon mustard
2 tablespoons dry cider
1 egg, beaten
salt and freshly ground black pepper
4 thick slices granary bread

1. Preheat the grill.

2. In a medium-sized bowl, mix together the Cheddar and Parmesan cheeses, the grated pear, mustard and cider.

3. Season the mixture with salt and black pepper, and add enough beaten egg to bind.

4. Toast the bread on both sides. Divide the cheese mixture between the slices, spreading right up to the edges.

5. Return to the grill for 1 minute.

6. Reduce the heat and continue to grill for a further 3–4 minutes or until the cheese has browned. Serve hot.

HOT SMOKED SALMON IN DILL AND LEMON BREAD

These delicious hot sandwiches make a perfect lunchtime snack – they are simple to make, easy to eat and very moreish. They can be completely prepared in advance and then baked at the last minute.

Preparation time: 10 minutes
Cooking time: 10 minutes
Serves 4 for lunch

*110g/4oz unsalted butter,
    softened*
zest of 2 lemons, finely grated
juice of 1 lemon
2 tablespoons dill, finely chopped
*salt and freshly ground black
    pepper*

2 baguettes
170g/6oz smoked salmon

To serve
cream cheese or crème fraîche

To garnish
sprigs of dill
lemon wedges

1. Preheat the oven to 200°C/400°F/gas mark 6.
2. Beat together the butter, lemon zest and juice and chopped dill until smooth. Season with salt and pepper.
3. Split the baguettes horizontally, taking care not to cut right through them. Spread two-thirds of the butter on the cut sides of each loaf and sandwich back together. Spread the remaining butter over the surface of the bread.
4. Wrap each baguette tightly in tinfoil and bake on the top shelf of the oven for 15 minutes or until hot through and crisp.
5. Remove the tinfoil and slightly open the baguettes. Arrange the smoked salmon in folds down the centre of each, and return to the oven for 5 minutes.
6. Cut each baguette in half widthwise and serve immediately, garnished with sprigs of dill, lemon wedges and a large spoonful of cream cheese or crème fraîche.

ROCKET SALSA BRUSCHETTA

Rocket can be expensive to buy but it is very easy to grow. You don't need to plant a great deal at a time, as it grows very quickly – with a bit of planning you can easily have fresh rocket available all summer. Most supermarkets sell very good-quality ciabatta.

The salsa can be prepared well in advance but the ciabatta should be grilled at the last minute.

Bruschetta make excellent first courses, snacks or canapés – simply cut the ciabatta to appropriate sizes.

Preparation time: 15 minutes
Cooking time: 5 minutes
Serves 4

For the salsa
140g/5oz rocket, washed and coarsely chopped
2 tablespoons extra virgin olive oil
½ small red onion, very finely chopped
1 tablespoon balsamic vinegar
2 ripe plum tomatoes, deseeded and very finely chopped
10 Kalamata olives, pitted and chopped

salt and freshly ground black pepper

For the bruschetta
2 ciabatta rolls, split horizontally in half
2 tablespoons extra virgin olive oil
2 tablespoons Parmesan cheese, freshly grated

1. Mix together all the ingredients for the salsa and season well with salt and freshly ground black pepper. Set aside.
2. Drizzle the olive oil over the cut side of the ciabatta rolls and grill lightly until golden brown.
3. Sprinkle the Parmesan cheese on the toasted rolls, and grill again until the cheese just begins to colour.
4. Divide the rocket salsa between the rolls and serve immediately, while the ciabatta is still warm.

DILL AND WHOLEGRAIN MUSTARD SCONES WITH SMOKED SALMON AND CREAM CHEESE

This is a variation on the theme of bagels with smoked salmon and cream cheese. The scones are quick to make and the flavour of the dill and mustard complements the smoked salmon, lime and cream cheese. They can be eaten for brunch, as a snack or as a first course. Do buy good-quality smoked salmon – the cheaper versions can taste very oily.

Preparation time: 15 minutes
Cooking time: 10 minutes
Serves 6

225g/8oz self-raising flour
½ teaspoon salt
55g/2oz butter
1½ tablespoons dill, finely chopped
1½ tablespoons wholegrain mustard
150ml/¼ pint buttermilk
1 egg, beaten, for glazing

To serve
110g/4oz sliced smoked salmon
55g/2oz cream cheese
1 tablespoon lime juice
zest of 1 lime, grated
freshly ground black pepper
1 lime, cut into 6 wedges

1. Set the oven to 220°C/425°F/gas mark 7. Flour a baking sheet.
2. Sift the flour and salt into a large bowl.
3. Rub in the butter until the mixture resembles breadcrumbs. Stir in the dill.
4. Mix the wholegrain mustard with the buttermilk. Make a deep well in the centre of the flour, pour in all the liquid and mix with a knife to a soft, spongy dough.
5. On a floured surface, knead the dough very lightly until just smooth. Roll out to about 2.5cm/1in thick and stamp into small rounds using a pastry cutter.
6. Brush the scones with beaten egg.
7. Bake the scones at the top of the preheated oven for 7 minutes or until well risen and brown.
8. Mix together the cream cheese, lime juice and zest and season to taste with black pepper.
9. Serve the scones warm with the smoked salmon, cream cheese and a wedge of lime.

HOT BRIE, APPLE AND ROCKET CIABATTA

This delicious hot sandwich can be prepared a couple of hours in advance and then baked at the last minute. It makes for a delicious snack-style supper ideal for the Christmas holidays.

Preparation time: 10 minutes
Cooking time: 20 minutes
Serves 4

1 Cox's apple, quartered, cored and chopped
3 tablespoons sweet white wine
freshly ground black pepper
225g/8oz Brie cheese, thinly sliced
85g/3oz pecan nuts, roughly chopped
85g/3oz rocket leaves, roughly torn
1 ciabatta loaf, cut horizontally in half

1. Preheat the oven to 200°C/400°F/gas mark 6.
2. Pour the white wine over the apple quarters and season with black pepper.
3. Arrange the Brie on the bottom half of the ciabatta and cover with the pecan nuts, apple quarters and rocket.
4. Cover with the top half of the ciabatta and press down firmly. Wrap the sandwich tightly in tinfoil and place on a baking sheet. Put the sandwich on to the top shelf of the preheated oven and bake for 15 minutes. Leave to stand for 5 minutes before unwrapping. Slice thickly and serve immediately.

CRANBERRY AND BRIE CANAPÉS

These canapés are very simple to make. Try to buy a good-quality cranberry sauce and use ripe Brie. They can be prepared in advance and then grilled at the last minute.

Preparation time: 5 minutes
Cooking time: 5 minutes
Makes: 15–20

1 French baton or flute　　　　　*300g/11oz Brie, sliced*
85g/3oz cranberry sauce　　　　*black pepper*

1. Heat the grill to a medium setting.
2. Cut the bread on the diagonal into 1.5cm/¾ in slices. Place the bread slices on to a baking sheet and place under the grill. Toast on both sides.
3. Spread the toast one side of each toasted slice with some cranberry sauce and put the slices of Brie over the top, making sure that none of the toast remains exposed. Sprinkle with a little black pepper. Put the baking sheet back underneath the grill until the Brie has melted. Serve immediately.

BALTIMORE CRAB CAKES

These crab cakes should ideally be made with fresh crabmeat, but canned or frozen will do. The inclusion of mayonnaise adds an excellent texture but means that the cakes cannot be frozen. They can, however, be made a day in advance and grilled when required. If you can't get hold of Old Bay spice, use Tabasco in its place.

Preparation time: 20 minutes
Cooking time: 8–10 minutes
Serves 6

225g/8oz brown and white　　*salt and freshly ground black*
　　crabmeat　　　　　　　　　　*pepper*
110g/4oz fresh white　　　　　*1 teaspoon Old Bay seasoning (if*
　　breadcrumbs　　　　　　　　　　*obtainable)*
150ml/¼ pint mayonnaise
1 bunch spring onions, chopped　*To serve*
1 tablespoon parsley, chopped　*green salad*
1 teaspoon horseradish sauce　*sourdough bread*
3–5 drops Tabasco sauce

1. Preheat the grill to its highest setting.
2. Mix together all of the ingredients except for a third of the breadcrumbs, and shape into 4 large or 8 small patties/cakes.
3. Dip the cakes in the remaining breadcrumbs and place on a lipped baking sheet. Grill for 8–10 minutes, without turning over, until golden brown.
4. Serve with a green salad and sourdough bread.

SMOKED HADDOCK AND CAPER FISH CAKES

These fish cakes can be made in advance and then frozen and fried when required. If poaching the haddock yourself, reserve the poaching milk and if it doesn't taste too salty use it to make the mashed potato. The reason these fish cakes are particularly good is the addition of chopped hard-boiled eggs and capers. They don't need an accompanying sauce – simply serve with lemon wedges.

Preparation time: 30 minutes
Cooking time: 10 minutes
Serves 4

285g/10oz smoked haddock, poached and flaked, bones removed
200g/7oz mashed potato
1 hard-boiled egg, roughly chopped
1 tablespoon freshly chopped parsley
1 tablespoon capers, drained, well rinsed and roughly chopped

salt and freshly ground black pepper
1 egg, beaten for binding
dry white breadcrumbs
oil for frying

To serve
dressed green salad
lemon wedges

1. Mix together the haddock, mashed potato, hard-boiled egg and capers. Season with plenty of black pepper and salt (you may not need the salt).
2. Add enough beaten egg to bind the mixture so that it is soft but not sloppy.
3. Shape the mixture into 8 2.5cm/1in-thick cakes. Brush with more of the beaten egg and coat in the breadcrumbs.
4. Heat the oil in a heavy-based frying pan and fry the cakes until brown all over.
5. Serve with a dressed green salad and lemon wedges.

SESAME PRAWN TOASTS

These delicious toasts can be served as a first course or as a canapé.
The prawn paste can be made in advance and then frozen. Once the
toasts have been assembled they should be fried reasonably quickly.
The same recipe can be made using minced chicken or pork in place of
the prawns – you may well like to add some soy sauce to the minced
chicken or pork.

Preparation time: 15 minutes
Cooking time: 1 minute
Makes 20

140g/5oz raw tiger prawns,   *large pinch of salt*
  peeled and deveined   *5 slices white bread*
1 tablespoon egg white   *2–3 tablespoons sesame seeds*
1 heaped teaspoon cornflour   *oil for deep-frying*

1. Put the prawns, egg whites, cornflour and salt into a food processor or
blender. Whizz to a paste.
2. Cut the crusts off the bread. Spread the prawn paste evenly over the slices
of bread and press a generous quantity of sesame seeds on top. Cut the slices
of bread in half, and then cut each half into 4 triangles or short fingers.
3. Heat the oil in a deep-fryer or heavy-based saucepan, until a crumb will
brown in 15 seconds.
4. Fry the sesame-seed toasts, prawn-side down, a few at a time in the hot
oil for 10–15 seconds, then flip them over and fry for a further 10–15
seconds. They should be golden brown all over. Drain on absorbent paper
and serve immediately.

TIGER PRAWNS WITH GARLIC BREAD

This makes a quick, light supper dish that is particularly good served
with baby red chard. Most supermarkets now sell raw tiger prawns –
they are generally very much nicer than ready-cooked prawns. Having
tested this recipe using both ciabatta rolls and baguettes, we are agreed
that ciabatta are preferable when given the choice.

Preparation time: 30 minutes
Cooking time: 10 minutes
Serves 4

170g/6oz *unsalted butter*
3 *large cloves garlic, peeled and*
  crushed
4 *ciabatta rolls or small baguettes*
24 *large raw tiger prawns*
salt and freshly ground black
  pepper

1 tablespoon *white wine or lemon*
  juice
good handful of flat-leaf parsley,
  chopped

To serve
1 *lemon, cut into wedges*
baby red chard

1. Preheat the oven to 200°C/400°F/gas mark 6.
2. Melt the butter in a large frying pan. Add the crushed garlic and fry gently for 1 minute. Turn off the heat and leave to infuse for 5–10 minutes.
3. Put the bread rolls on to a baking sheet and place in the centre of the oven for 5 minutes.
4. Peel and devein the prawns, discarding the shells.
5. Reheat the garlic butter, add the prawns to the pan and cook over a medium heat for 2–3 minutes or until the prawns turn pink. Season with salt and black pepper, add the white wine or lemon juice and stir in the parsley.
6. Split the warm rolls horizontally in half and put 2 halves on to each of 4 serving plates. Top with the prawns and pour the sizzling garlic butter over the top. Serve immediately with the lemon wedges, garnished with baby red chard.

THAI-STYLE PRAWN KEBABS

The prawns should be marinated for as long as possible – up to 24 hours – to allow the flavours to permeate the prawns. If fresh lemon grass is not available, dried is a suitable alternative. This recipe calls for the use of wooden skewers; before assembling the kebabs, soak the skewers in cold water for at least 20 minutes (this will prevent them from burning under the grill). This marinade can also be used for chicken breasts.

Preparation time: 25 minutes
Cooking time: 5–6 minutes
Serves 4

4 tablespoons oil
2 tablespoons ginger wine
½ red chilli, finely chopped
1 kaffir lime leaf, bruised
   (optional)
1 stick lemon grass, bruised
½ tablespoon fresh coriander,
   chopped
1 clove garlic, crushed

black pepper
16 raw tiger prawns, peeled and
   deveined, tails left on
   juice of half a lime

To serve
coriander sprigs
lime wedges

1. Put the oil, ginger wine, chilli, lime leaf (if using), lemon grass, coriander, garlic, and black pepper, into a bowl and stir well. Add the prawns, stir well and leave to marinate for as long as possible, basting occasionally.
2. Preheat the grill to a high temperature. Squeeze the lime juice over the prawns and stir, then thread 4 prawns on to each skewer. Place the skewers on a baking sheet and cook under the grill for about 3 minutes on each side, basting with the marinade as necessary.
3. When the prawns are cooked, serve immediately, garnished with the fresh coriander and lime wedges.

TROUT GRAVAD LAX

This is a simple variation on the classic gravad lax, which is made from a whole pickled salmon. In this recipe we have used trout fillets, which means that you can easily vary the quantity you make depending on the number of people that you are serving. This recipe is for a main course for 4 people – if serving it as a first course, 2 trout should be plenty.

Preparation time: 15 minutes plus 12 hours marinating
Serves 4

4 rainbow trout, filleted, skinned
   and pinboned
85g/3oz sea salt
85g/3oz caster sugar
freshly ground white pepper
small bunch dill, chopped

To serve
mustard and dill sauce:
½ tablespoon Dijon mustard
3 tablespoons oil
1 tablespoon wine vinegar
½ tablespoon chopped fresh dill
salt and freshly ground black
   pepper

1. Mix together the salt, sugar, pepper and dill and spread half the mixture in a large flat dish. Lay the trout on top in a single layer. Cover with the remaining salt mixture. Cover tightly and refrigerate for 12 hours or overnight.
2. Meanwhile, make the sauce: put the mustard into a small bowl and gradually whisk in the oil, then the vinegar. Mix in the dill and season to taste with salt and pepper.
3. Wash the trout well and pat dry on absorbent paper.
4. Serve the trout with the mustard and dill sauce.

SMOKED MACKEREL PÂTÉ

This is a delicious basic recipe that can also be made using other smoked oily fish, such as trout, salmon or eel. The gherkins and capers add some necessary piquancy; if you don't like them, use a little creamed horseradish instead.

Preparation and chilling time: 20 minutes
Serves 4

4 smoked mackerel fillets, skinned
6 tablespoons crème fraîche
2 teaspoons lemon juice
30g/1oz capers, rinsed, drained
   and chopped
30g/1oz gherkins, rinsed, drained
   and chopped

salt and freshly ground black
   pepper

To serve
melba toast
green salad

1. Place the mackerel fillets, crème fraîche and lemon juice in a food processor or blender and pulse until combined.

2. Turn the mixture into a bowl and add the capers, gherkins and season with salt and pepper. Combine well and turn into 4 ramekins. Keep covered and chilled until ready to serve.
3. Serve with melba toast and a green salad.

CHICKEN LIVER PÂTÉ

This delicious pâté is making a revival. We have cut down on some of the butter that is in other recipes, and added crème fraîche to make it lighter. You can further cut down on the butter if required – half-fat crème fraîche can be used in place of the full-fat version. Chicken livers are very good value, so this recipe is economic, too. Check over the livers well and remove any discoloured pieces as they will taste bitter, rinse under cold water and drain before frying. If the pâté is to be kept for more than 3 days, cover the top with a layer of clarified butter. The pâté will not set solid, so it is very easy to spread.

Preparation time: 15 minutes
Cooking time: 10 minutes
Serves 4–6

85g/3oz butter
1 large onion
1 clove garlic, crushed (optional)
450g/1lb chicken livers

2 tablespoons brandy
4 tablespoons crème fraîche
salt and pepper

1. Melt half the butter in a large heavy frying pan and gently fry the onion until soft and transparent.
2. Add the garlic, if using, and continue cooking for a further minute.
3. Add the livers to the pan and fry, turning to brown them lightly on all sides, until cooked. Flame the brandy and add to the livers.
4. When the flames subside, add salt and plenty of pepper.
5. Add the crème fraîche and liquidise in a food processor or blender with the remaining butter. Put it into an earthenware dish or pot.

POTTED SALMON

We emphasise the importance of being creative with leftover ingredients to all our students at Leith's. This recipe is a delicious way of using up leftover from a whole poached fish. Alternatives to the salmon are cooked trout, crab, prawns and shrimp. Serve as a first-course or light lunch with melba toast or fresh bread.

Preparation time: 10 minutes
Serves 4

225g/8oz cooked salmon
85g/3oz butter, softened
1 tablespoon Worcester sauce
1 tablespoon anchovy essence
salt and freshly ground black pepper

½ teaspoon cayenne pepper
55g/2oz butter, clarified, melted
    and cooled

1. Remove any skin and bones from the salmon. Put it into a food processor or blender with the butter, Worcester sauce and anchovy essence, and whizz together to form a smooth paste.
2. Season to taste with salt and freshly ground black pepper and the cayenne pepper.
3. Pack the salmon paste into a soufflé dish or ramekin, making sure that it is packed down well. Smooth the top of the paste and pour the cold melted butter over the top. Refrigerate and use within 2 days.

SALMON EN CROÛTE

This quick and simple salmon en croûte recipe is made using ready-rolled puff pastry – make sure that the pastry you buy has been rolled to an oblong shape. We have given a cooking time of 30–35 minutes but you need to check that it has cooked on the bottom before removing it from the oven. Serve hot with new potatoes and a green salad or cold as part of a picnic dish.

Preparation time: 15 minutes
Cooking time: 30–35 minutes
Serves 8

1 × 500g/1lb 1oz packet puff pastry
900g/2lb salmon fillet, skinned and pinboned
300g/11oz soft garlic and herb cheese
1 egg, beaten

1. Preheat the oven to 200°C/400°F/gas mark 6.
2. Roll out the pastry to the thickness of a 20p coin. It should be slightly larger than an A4 sheet of paper.
3. Season the salmon well and spread a generous layer of the garlic and herb creamy cheese over the fillet, on the skinned side.
4. Lay the salmon fillet, cheese-side down, in the centre of the rolled-out pastry.
5. Wrap the pastry around the salmon and seal with the egg glaze. There should be a small overlap.
6. Place on a baking sheet, sealed-side down, and make 2 diagonal slashes through the top of the pastry. Brush with egg glaze.
7. Chill in the refridgerator for 15 minutes, then bake in the oven for 30–35 minutes until the pastry is golden brown.

SMOKED HADDOCK AND SPINACH RISOTTO

This recipe uses partly cooked commercially prepared risotto rice, which means that you can cook risotto for a dinner party or casual supper without having to spend the last half an hour in the kitchen.

Preparation time: 10 minutes
Cooking time: 12 minutes
Serves 2

1 × 250g/8½oz packet saffron
  risotto rice
170g/6oz smoked haddock
170g/6oz baby spinach, washed
  and destalked

30g/1oz Parmesan cheese, freshly
  grated
salt and ground black pepper

1. Place the risotto rice in a large pan and add water as per the packet instructions.
2. Bring to the boil and cook for 10 minutes, stirring occasionally.
3. Cut the smoked haddock into bite-sized pieces and add to the rice. Stir gently and cook for 2 minutes.
4. Gently stir in the spinach, taking care not to break up the fish. Cook until the spinach just wilts.
5. Season to taste with salt and pepper. Serve immediately with the freshly grated Parmesan.

SEARED TUNA SALAD WITH CAPERS AND RED ONION

This is a very simple first course that can be made at the last minute or prepared in advance. In fact the dressing will improve if made earlier – the onion will soften a little in the oil. It is essential that the onion is very finely chopped and that the capers are well rinsed. The best capers are generally those packed in salt.

Preparation time: 5 minutes
Cooking time: 7 minutes
Serves 6 as a first course

450g/1lb loin of tuna in one piece
5 tablespoons olive oil
1 small red onion, very finely chopped
2 tablespoons capers, drained and
  rinsed well

1 tablespoon lemon juice
1 packet rocket
salt and freshly ground black
  pepper

1. Rub the tuna with salt and pepper, then rub with 2 tablespoons of the olive oil.
2. Heat a heavy-based frying pan until very hot and sear the tuna on each side for 20–30 seconds to seal rather than cook. Leave to rest for 5 minutes.
3. Mix the onion with the capers. Add the remaining oil and the lemon juice. Season.
4. Divide the rocket between 6 plates. Slice the tuna thinly. Arrange on the rocket and pour the dressing over the top.

FISH GOUJONS WITH HONEY AND LEMON MAYONNAISE

Goujons are traditionally served with tartare sauce but this honey and lemon mayonnaise gives a refreshingly different flavour. Choose a firm-fleshed fish such as a sole for the goujons.

Preparation time: 10 minutes
Cooking time: 5–10 minutes

110g/4oz per person white-fish
  fillets, skinned
oil for deep-frying
seasoned plain flour
beaten egg
dried white crumbs
salt

For the mayonnaise
1 tablespoon honey
1 tablespoon lemon juice
150ml/¼ pint mayonnaise
zest of half a lemon

1. Make the mayonnaise: put the honey into a bowl, stir in the lemon juice and zest and add the mayonnaise.
2. Cut the fish across the grain or on the diagonal into finger-like strips.
3. Heat the oil in a deep-fryer until a crumb will sizzle in it.
4. Dip the fish into the seasoned flour, then into the beaten egg, and toss to coat with the breadcrumbs.
5. Fry a few goujons at a time until crisp and golden brown. Drain well on absorbent kitchen paper and sprinkle with salt. Serve with the honey and lemon mayonnaise.

SOY-GLAZED TUNA WITH HOT AND SOUR SALAD

This recipe calls for tuna fish but it can also be made with salmon fillets. When we tested this recipe it was universally popular with all the staff. It is very quick and easy to make and looks very attractive. The longer the fish remains in the marinade, the better. It can be prepared in advance but cook the fish and combine the salad ingredients at the last minute. Serve with new potatoes.

Preparation and marinating time: 1 hour
Cooking time: 5 minutes
Serves 4

4 × 170g/6oz tuna steaks

For the marinade
5 tablespoons soy sauce
1 tablespoon sesame oil
1 teaspoon honey

For the hot and sour dressing
3 tablespoons rice wine vinegar
1 red chilli, finely chopped
1 tablespoon caster sugar
1 tablespoon sunflower oil
140g/5oz cashew nuts

1 teaspoon sea salt crystals (Malden if available)
1 teaspoon black mustard seeds

For the salad
225g/8oz beansprouts
110g/4oz mangetout, roughly chopped
1 small can water chestnuts, drained and sliced
zest and juice of 1 lime
1 tablespoon chopped fresh coriander

1. Combine the marinade ingredients and pour the mixture over the tuna steaks. Leave for up to 1 hour.
2. Make the hot and sour dressing: place the vinegar, chilli and sugar in a small saucepan and heat gently, without boiling, until the sugar has dissolved. Leave to cool and then add the sunflower oil.
3. Gently fry the cashew nuts in a heavy-based frying pan until lightly browned, then add the sea salt and mustard seeds and fry for 1 minute, or until the seeds start to pop. Set aside.
4. In a hot pan, fry the tuna steaks for 4 minutes on each side – it shouldn't be necessary to add any extra oil to the pan.
5. Combine all the salad ingredients together and toss in the dressing and pile on to each of 4 plates. Top each pile with the soy-glazed tuna and serve.

PAN-FRIED LIME AND PARSLEY COD STEAKS WITH SALT AND VINEGAR CHIPS

This is a slightly trendy, healthy imitation of fish and chips – and there is no deep-frying involved, so no smell or mess. The hot roasted potatoes quickly absorb the vinegar, giving them a delicious flavour while the sea salt adds to their crisp texture.

Preparation time: 20 minutes
Cooking time: 1 hour
Serves 4

675g/1½lb potatoes
7 tablespoons olive oil
coarse sea salt and freshly ground
  black pepper
4 tablespoons balsamic vinegar
4 tablespoons dried white
  breadcrumbs
zest of 3 limes, finely grated

small handful of flat-leaf parsley,
  chopped
4 × 170g/6oz cod steaks, skinned
1 egg, beaten

To serve
lime wedges
flat-leaf parsley

1. Set the oven to 200°C/400°F/gas mark 6.
2. Wash the potatoes and cut each one into 6 wedges, lengthways, and put them into a roasting tin. Cover with 3 tablespoons of the olive oil. Season with plenty of sea salt and black pepper.
3. Put the roasting tin into the top of the oven and cook, turning occasionally, for 50–60 minutes or until the potatoes are crisp and brown. Add the balsamic vinegar to the tin, and return to the oven for a further 5 minutes.
4. Meanwhile, prepare the cod: mix together the dried breadcrumbs, lime zest and parsley in a bowl and season with salt and black pepper.
5. Dip the fish into the beaten egg, and then press the crumb mixture firmly on to both sides.
6. Heat the remaining oil in a frying pan, and when hot fry the fish on both sides until well browned. Reduce the heat and cook for a further 5–7 minutes or until the fish is cooked through. (The exact cooking time will depend on the thickness of the fish.)
7. Make a pile of the salt and vinegar chips on each of 4 warmed serving plates, placing a piece of cod on top. Drizzle the potato juices around the fish, garnish with a wedge of lime and sprig of parsley and serve at once.

MONKFISH PARCELS

This method of cooking fish (en papilotte) is excellent because all the moisture is contained within the parcel, making for a very tender, succulent piece of fish. The final appearance is rustic rather than elegant but, if preferred, the monkfish can be removed from the parcel, the chilli, garlic, lemon grass and lime leaves can be discarded and the fish can be served sprinkled with the roughly chopped coriander. The monkfish can be substituted with other types of white fish, but the cooking time may need to be adjusted. The cream can also be omitted, but the final result will be hotter.

Preparation: 15 minutes
Cooking time: 10 minutes
Serves 4

4 × 140g/5oz monkfish tail fillets
190ml/⅓ pint ginger wine
1 red chilli, sliced on the diagonal
2 cloves garlic, peeled and halved
1 stick lemon grass, bruised and
  cut into 4
2 kaffir lime leaves, broken in
  half (optional)
juice of 1 lime
oil for greasing

4 tablespoons double cream or
  coconut cream
salt and freshly ground black
  pepper

To garnish
1 tablespoon roughly chopped
  fresh coriander

To serve
Stick rice or noodles

1. Trim the monkfish fillets of all membrane; this should be done meticulously.
2. Put the monkfish into a bowl with the ginger wine, chilli, garlic, lemon grass, and the kaffir lime leaves if using. Stir and cover, then allow to marinate in the refrigerator for several hours, turning occasionally.
3. Preheat the oven to 200°C/400°F/gas mark 6.
4. Add the lime juice to the marinade and stir thoroughly.
5. Cut 4 large squares of tinfoil, brush lightly with oil and place a piece of monkfish in the centre of each square. Season with a little salt and pepper and divide the marinade ingredients between the parcels, so that each parcel has a piece of lemon grass, chilli, etc.
6. Put a spoonful of cream into each parcel, then seal tightly, but allow some room for steam.
7. Put onto a baking sheet and cook in the oven for 15 minutes.

8. Open the parcels, sprinkle the chopped coriander over the fish, and reseal.
9. Serve immediately, in the sealed tinfoil, so that your guests can open them at the table, with sticky rice or noodles.

COD WITH WARM TARTARE DRESSING

This is a variation of a classic fish dish but is simpler as it requires no batter-making or deep-fat frying. It is worth buying good-quality capers – the Italian salted ones are far superior to the ones in brine. The tartare sauce can be made a day in advance but the fish must, of course, be cooked at the last minute.

Preparation time: 10 minutes
Cooking time: 10 minutes
Serves 4

4 × 170g/6oz cod fillets, skin on
salt and freshly ground black pepper
flour
2 tablespoons oil

55g/2oz capers, rinsed, diced and
  chopped
zest of 2 limes, finely grated
4 tablespoons mayonnaise

For the dressing
1 shallot, very finely chopped
55g/2oz cornichons or dill pickles,
  rinsed, diced and chopped

To serve
2 tablespoons flat leaf
  parsley

1. Season the fish with salt and black pepper and dust the skin side lightly with a little flour. Heat the oil in a large frying pan and fry the fish, skin-side down, until brown.
2. Reduce the heat and cook the other side of the fish for a further 2–3 minutes or until cooked through.
3. Meanwhile, in a small bowl mix together all the dressing ingredients and season with salt and black pepper. Heat gently in a small saucepan.
4. Place the fish on a plate, skin-side up. Garnish with parsley and serve, handing the warm tartare sauce separately.

SALMON WITH MUSTARD AND BRANDY SAUCE

This easy salmon dish should be served with rice and a green salad. We recommend cooking rice in a rice cooker to guarantee perfect results every time.

Preparation time: 15 minutes
Cooking time: 10 minutes
Serves 4–6

30g/1oz unsalted butter
4 × 170g/6oz salmon fillet, skinned,
    boned and cut into 2cm/1in cubes
2 tablespoons plain flour
1 shallot, finely chopped
1 clove garlic, crushed
450g/1lb button mushrooms,
    trimmed, wiped and cut in half

2 tablespoons brandy
1 tablespoon Dijon mustard
225ml/7½fl oz double cream
4 tablespoons water
1 tablespoon finely chopped
    parsley
salt and freshly ground pepper

1. Heat half of the butter in a large frying pan. Toss the cubes of salmon in the plain flour, shake off any excess, then fry gently until lightly golden but not cooked through. Remove from the pan with a slotted spoon.
2. Add the shallot to the pan with the rest of the butter, and cook gently for 2 minutes. Add the garlic and cook for 30 seconds. Add the mushrooms, cover with a lid and cook for 5 minutes or until soft. Remove the lid, turn up the heat and cook, stirring until the mushrooms start to sizzle.
3. Add the brandy, Dijon mustard, cream and water. Bring to the boil, stirring constantly, scraping any sediment from the bottom of the pan. Stir in the salmon and parsley and season with salt and pepper. Serve with rice and a green salad.

PAN-FRIED SWORDFISH STEAKS WITH MUSTARD BUTTER AND BASIL

This pan-fried swordfish dish is fantastically simple to make. If swordfish is not available, use marlin or tuna fish instead – it needs to be a firm-textured fish. If you have one, frying the fish on a griddle will make it more attractive.

Preparation time: 10 minutes
Cooking time: 10 minutes
Serves 4

55g/2oz butter, softened
2 teaspoons grainy mustard
salt and freshly ground black pepper
4 × 170g/6oz swordfish steaks,
  skinned

salt and freshly ground black pepper
juice of ½ lemon
2 tablespoons chopped basil

To serve
basil sprigs

1. Cream the butter until very soft, beat in the mustard and season with salt and pepper.
2. Season the swordfish steaks with salt and pepper.
3. Melt half the mustard butter in a frying pan. When it is foaming, fry 2 swordfish steaks over a gentle heat for 3 minutes on each side or until the fish is lightly browned and cooked (the flesh should be opaque and firm). Do not allow the butter to get so hot that it burns. Lift out the fish and keep warm. Melt the remaining butter and cook the remaining 2 steaks in the same way.
4. Arrange the swordfish steaks on a serving dish.
5. Add the lemon juice, basil, salt and pepper to the pan. While the butter is still sizzling, pour it over the swordfish. Garnish with a few sprigs of basil and serve.

85

THAI MUSSELS

There is a wonderful element of surprise in this dish – it looks like moules marinières but tastes wonderfully exotic as the flavour of the curry paste permeates right through to the centre of the mussels. Mussels are best cooked in a steamy atmosphere beneath a tight-fitting lid. Serve with plenty of French bread.

Preparation time: 15 minutes
Cooking time: 10 minutes
Serves 4

2kg/4lb mussels
2 tablespoons oil
2 medium onions, very finely
chopped
1 clove garlic, crushed
1½ tablespoons red Thai curry paste
150ml/¼ pint water
150ml/¼ pint coconut milk

1 tablespoon chopped fresh coriander
salt and freshly ground black pepper

To serve
2 tablespoons fresh coriander, roughly chopped

1. Clean the mussels by scrubbing them well under a running tap. Pull away the 'beards' (seaweed-like threads). Throw away any mussels that are cracked or that remain open when tapped.
2. Heat the oil in a large deep pan, add the onion and sweat until soft but not coloured. Add the garlic and the curry paste and continue to cook for 45 seconds, then add the water, coconut milk and coriander and bring up to simmering point.
3. Add the mussels, put on the lid and leave to steam over a low heat, shaking the pan occasionally, for about 5 minutes or until all the shells have opened. Tip the mussels into a colander set over a bowl, reserving the liquid.
4. Throw away any mussels that have not opened. Pour the mussel liquid into a saucepan. Boil and reduce well, and season to taste with salt and pepper. If the sauce is too spicy, add a little more coconut milk.
5. Transfer the mussels to a warmed soup tureen or wide bowl. Pour the sauce over the mussels, sprinkle with the fresh coriander and serve immediately.

SMOKED HADDOCK KEDGEREE

Kedgeree originated in India and was Anglicised in the eighteenth century with the addition of smoked fish. Nowadays it is traditionally served for breakfast but it also makes an excellent lunch or supper dish. Try to buy the best smoked haddock you can – the flavour of the fish can vary enormously depending on the quality.

The kedgeree can be completely prepared in advance and then reheated in the oven instead of on the stove – it will not spoil if reheated at a low temperature (130°C/250°F/gas mark 1) – but it does not freeze well. This recipe calls for smoked haddock but it is very good when made with fresh salmon. Chopped parsley can also make a delicious addition. Although the recipe is easy to make, it can go wrong – particularly if you don't use enough butter, because the rice will then taste horribly dry. It is also very important to season the kedgeree well.

Preparation time: 15 minutes
Cooking time: 5 minutes
Serves 4

85g/3oz butter
140g/5oz (raw weight) long-grain rice, boiled
340g/12oz smoked haddock fillet, cooked, skinned and boned
3 hard-boiled eggs, roughly chopped
salt and freshly ground black pepper
cayenne pepper

1. Melt the butter in a large shallow saucepan and add all the remaining ingredients.
2. Stir gently until very hot.
3. Turn on to a large dish and garnish with a further sprinkling of cayenne pepper.

SMOKED HADDOCK WITH RAREBIT CRUST

This is the ultimate cheese on toast – it is simple to make, tastes delicious and can be prepared well in advance. Serve with grilled tomatoes and a green vegetable, such as garden peas. If you have a blowtorch you can use that instead of the grill to brown the rarebit.

Preparation time: 5 minutes plus ½ hour chilling
Cooking time: 15 minutes
Serves 4

110g/4oz *Gruyère cheese, finely*
  grated
110g/4oz *Cheddar cheese, finely*
  grated
4 *teaspoons French mustard*
salt and freshly ground black pepper

cayenne pepper
2 *eggs, beaten*
2 *tablespoons beer*
4 × 170g/6oz *fillet pieces of*
  smoked haddock, pinboned

1. Mix the cheeses together with the mustard, salt, pepper, cayenne, egg and beer.
2. Spread the rarebit mixture neatly over the haddock fillets, up to the edges, and refrigerate for 30 minutes.
3. Preheat the oven to 190°C/375°F/gas mark 5.
4. Place the haddock in a roasting tin and bake for 15 minutes.
5. Meanwhile, preheat the grill to its highest setting.
6. Remove the fish from the oven.
7. If the rarebit has not yet browned, place under the grill until it has. Serve immediately.

SALMON BAKED WITH A SWEET AND HOT CRUST

This is an ideal recipe for a dinner party. It can be completely prepared in advance and then baked at the last minute. Serve with new potatoes and a green salad.

Preparation time: 10 minutes
Cooking time: 15 minutes
Serves 6

1.1kg/2½lb *salmon fillet, skinned*
oil for brushing
1 *tablespoon of demerara sugar*
½ *teaspoon dry English mustard*
zest of 3 limes or 2 lemons, finely
  grated

2 *tablespoons grainy mustard*
6 *tablespoons dried*
  breadcrumbs
pinch of cayenne pepper

To garnish
Watercress

1. Preheat the oven to 190°C/375°F/gas mark 5.
2. Trim the salmon fillet and remove any bones.
3. Mix together the remaining ingredients to make the crust.
4. Press the mixture over the salmon. Cut into 6 even pieces, place on a lightly oiled baking sheet and bake in the oven for 15 minutes.
5. Garnish the salmon with bouquets of watercress and serve immediately.

SALMON WITH GINGER AND ORANGE

This is a very quick and easy dish that can be prepared well in advance and then cooked at the last minute. Serve it with mashed potatoes and a green vegetable. A jar of stem ginger is very useful to keep in the refrigerator. The syrup can be used to add zest to sauces and the ginger itself can be added to a variety of leftover dishes.

Preparation time: 10 minutes
Cooking time: 6 minutes
Serves 4

4 × 170g/6oz salmon fillets,
  skinned and pinboned
salt and freshly ground black
  pepper

4 pieces stem ginger
juice and grated zest of 1 orange
2 tablespoons syrup from stem
  ginger

1. Place the salmon fillets in a large bowl and sprinkle with salt and pepper.
2. Cut the stem ginger into fine julienne sticks and put into the bowl with the salmon. Add the orange zest.
3. Mix the orange juice with the ginger syrup and pour the mixture over the salmon. Cover and refrigerate for at least 1 hour.
4. Heat the grill to its highest setting.
5. Grill the salmon on one side until crisp. Turn over and baste with the orange and ginger mixture. Grill the second side for about 5 minutes or until golden brown. Serve.

LAMB BURGERS WITH MINT AND CHERRY TOMATO SALSA

Lamb burgers make an interesting alternative to the traditional hamburgers – and they can, of course, be served in warmed baps. The lamb mixture can be prepared and shaped in advance and then frozen or cooked as required. The grated zest of an orange can be added to the lamb mixture or the salsa.

Preparation time: 10 minutes
Cooking time: 10 minutes
Serves 4

1 tablespoon oil
1 small onion, chopped
1 teaspoon ground cumin
450g/1lb minced lean lamb
1 tablespoon chopped fresh mint
1 tablespoon chopped fresh parsley
salt and pepper

For the salsa
1 small red onion, finely chopped
1 tablespoon balsamic vinegar
3 tablespoons good-quality olive oil
225g/8oz cherry tomatoes, halved
1 tablespoon chopped mint
salt and pepper

1. Preheat the grill.
2. Heat the oil in a saucepan. Add the onion and cook until soft but not coloured, then add the cumin and cook for 2 minutes. Remove from the heat and leave to cool.
3. When the onion is cold, mix with the lamb, mint and parsley. Mix well and season with salt and pepper.
4. With wet hands, shape the meat into flattish rounds, making sure that they are equal in size. Make a slight dip in the centre. The burgers will shrink and thicken when they cook.
5. Meanwhile, make the salsa: mix together the red onion, vinegar and oil and allow to stand for 10 minutes.
6. Grill the burgers steadily, turning once. Allow 3 minutes each side for rare burgers and 5 minutes each side to have them well done.
7. Add the tomatoes and mint to the red onions, taste and season with salt and pepper. Serve with the lamb burgers.

LAMB TAGINE

This is a simplified version of the famous Moroccan stew from Fez which is traditionally cooked in an earthenware pot called a tagine. It can be prepared with a variety of fruits and sometimes has honey and ginger added. We have used dried lime in this recipe but if you can get it use 2 strips of lime zest instead.

Preparation time: 15 minutes
Cooking time: 1 hour 40 minutes
Serves 4

3 tablespoons olive oil
900g/2lb boneless lamb, cut into
   2½cm/1in cubes, well trimmed
2 onions, chopped
2 cloves garlic, crushed
1 teaspoon ground ginger
1 teaspoon ground cinnamon
1 teaspoon ground cumin
860ml/1½ pints water or stock
2 tablespoons saffron tea

1 dried lime
110g/4oz 'no need to soak' dried
   stoned prunes
110g/4oz 'no need to soak'
   apricots

To serve
couscous
chopped fresh coriander

1. Heat 2 tablespoons of the oil in a heavy pan. Brown the lamb cubes well, a few at a time, removing them to a bowl as they are done. If the bottom of the pan becomes very dark or too dry, pour a little water into the pan and swish it about, then scrape off the sediment stuck to the pan bottom and pour the liquid over the removed meat.
2. When all the meat has been browned and put aside, heat the remaining tablespoon of oil, then add the onions and cook slowly for 5 minutes. Add the garlic and spices and cook for 1 minute.
3. Add the stock, saffron tea and lime, bring to the boil and return the meat to the pan. Season with salt and freshly ground black pepper and simmer slowly for 1½ hours. Add the prunes and apricots and cook for a further 10 minutes. Remove the lime before serving – or warn your guests about it.
4. Sprinkle the coriander over the lamb and serve with couscous.

LAMB STEAKS WITH ROAST BUTTER BEANS AND TOMATOES

This is a quick way to serve a truly hearty lamb dish, ideal for supper on a cold winter evening. Serve with potato wedges (cut baking potatoes into wedges, sprinkle with olive oil, crushed rosemary, salt and pepper and bake in a hot oven for 50 minutes) and a green vegetable. The tomato and butter bean mixture also goes well with pan-fried tuna steaks or chargrilled chicken breasts.

Preparation time: 15 minutes
Cooking time: 20 minutes
Serves 4

2 tablespoons extra virgin olive oil
2 × 400g/14oz can butter beans, rinsed and drained
4 ripe plum tomatoes, quartered
salt and freshly ground black pepper
1 tablespoon sunflower oil
4 × 170g/6oz thick-cut lamb leg steaks, trimmed

1 tablespoon sundried tomato paste
1½ tablespoons balsamic vinegar
55g/2oz coriander leaves, roughly chopped

To serve
coriander leaves

1. Preheat the oven to 200°C/400°F/gas mark 6.
2. In a large roasting tin heat the olive oil and stir in the butter beans and tomatoes. Season with salt and black pepper and roast on the top shelf of the oven for 5–10 minutes.
3. Meanwhile, heat the sunflower oil in a large frying pan, season the lamb steaks and brown them on both sides.

4. Remove the beans and tomatoes from the oven and stir in the sundried tomato paste and balsamic vinegar. Lay the lamb steaks and any pan juices on top and continue to cook for a further 5–7 minutes or until the lamb is pink in the middle.

5. Remove the lamb from the roasting tin and stir in the chopped coriander. Divide the beans and tomatoes between 4 warmed plates and put a lamb steak on top of each. Garnish with coriander leaves and serve.

ROGAN JOSH

This recipe is a Sri Lankan curry. Spices should be fried before they are incorporated into a dish – this serves to soften their harsh raw taste yet heighten their residual flavour. Rogan Josh should be red in colour, so the mild paprika is added at the end of the cooking time in order that it retains its redness. This recipe can be made in advance and then reheated or frozen as required.

Preparation time: 15 minutes
Cooking time: 50 minutes
Serves 4

675g/1½lb leg of lamb, boned
4 tablespoons oil
4 bay leaves
6 cardamom pods
5cm/2in cinnamon stick
6 cloves
1 medium onion, finely chopped
4 cloves garlic
5cm/2in piece of fresh root
  ginger, peeled
150ml/¼ pint plain yoghurt
1 teaspoon fennel seeds
2 teaspoons ground cumin
2 teaspoons ground coriander
1 teaspoon chilli powder
200ml/7fl oz water
salt
½ teaspoon garam masala
4 teaspoons paprika

1. Cut the lamb into 2.5cm/1in cubes. Reserve any bones.

2. Heat the oil in a medium saucepan and fry a few pieces of lamb at a time until browned. Reheat the oil after each batch, and add more oil as necessary.

3. Add the bay leaves, cardamom, cinnamon, cloves and onion to the pan and fry until the onion is lightly browned.

4. Mix together the garlic, ginger and yoghurt in a food processor or blender. Grind the fennel, cumin and coriander to a fine powder.

5. Add the ground spices to the onion in the pan. Add the lamb and any juices and stir until well mixed. Add the yoghurt mixture, chilli powder, water and salt to taste, and bring slowly to the boil. Cover, lower the heat and simmer for 30–40 minutes.
6. Just prior to serving, add the garam masala and paprika and heat through.

INDIAN SPICED LAMB BURGERS WITH MINI-NAAN

Spicy lamb burgers make a welcome change from beef on the summer barbecue. The burgers are easy to make and can be made up to 12 hours in advance of cooking or can be frozen for up to one month. This recipe uses mini-naan or pitta bread instead of burger buns and the burgers are garnished with chutney instead of tomato ketchup. Be sure to keep the mince icy cold until you are ready to cook. Serve with tomatoes and green salad.

Preparation time: 10 minutes
Cooking time: 5 minutes
Serves 4

450g/1lb lean minced lamb
2 tablespoons grated onion
2 tablespoons curry paste
2 tablespoons Greek yoghurt
2 tablespoons chopped fresh
 coriander or mint
1 scant teaspoon salt

4 mini-naan or pitta bread, split
 in half

To serve
4 tablespoons chutney (any
 flavour, but mango or lime are
 particularly suitable)
½ cucumber, sliced

1. Mix the lamb with the onion, curry paste, yoghurt, coriander or mint and salt.
2. With clean hands, form into 4 patties. Chill until required.
3. Light the barbecue, or preheat the grill to medium-high setting.
4. Wrap the bread in tinfoil and place on the barbecue or under the grill to warm through while the burgers are cooking.

5. Cook the burgers on the barbecue or under the grill for 2–3 minutes per side. They should be well browned on the outside and slightly pink inside.
6. Serve between the warmed, split bread, garnished with the chutney and cucumber slices.

ARMENIAN LAMB

This lamb stew can be made in advance and then frozen or reheated as required. In fact the flavour improves if the stew is made a day in advance and stored in the refridgerator. Serve with rice and a green vegetable.

Preparation time: 20 minutes
Cooking time: 1 hour
Serves 4–6

900g/2lb lamb (preferably from the shoulder)
2 tablespoons oil
2 medium onions, sliced
1 clove garlic, crushed
30g/1oz flour
1 teaspoon ground cumin
½ teaspoon allspice
1 tablespoon tomato purée
290ml/½ pint beef stock
salt and freshly ground black pepper

1. Trim the lamb and cut into 5cm/2in cubes.
2. Heat half the oil in a sauté pan and brown the meat a few pieces at a time. Remove the meat to a bowl.
3. Pour a little water into the pan, bring to the boil, scraping the bottom of the pan to loosen any sediment. Pour the liquid over the meat.
4. Heat the remaining oil in the pan, add the onions and cook slowly for 5 minutes. Add the garlic and cook for a further minute. Add the flour and spices and continue to cook for another 2 minutes.
5. Add the tomato purée and stock. Bring slowly to the boil, stirring constantly. Season with salt and pepper. Return the meat to the pan.
6. Simmer slowly for 45–60 minutes.

LAMB PITTA KEBABS

These are ideal for eating in a hurry – they are simply a warm sandwich filled with salad and warm lamb steaks. Like beef steaks, lamb can be eaten in any state from blue to well done. However, if overcooked they become very tough; they are best when pink in the middle. The longer the lamb marinates, the better the flavour will be.

Preparation time: 20 minutes (excluding marinating time)
Cooking time: 10 minutes
Serves 4

4 × 110g/4oz lamb steaks,
  trimmed
3 tablespoons oil
1 tablespoon chopped fresh
  rosemary
zest of 1 lemon
salt and freshly ground black
  pepper

1 small bag bistro salad
2 tablespoons salad dressing
8 pitta breads

To serve (optional)
chilli dipping sauce
soured cream

1. Put the lamb steaks into a shallow bowl and cover with the oil, rosemary and lemon zest and season with black pepper. Allow to marinate for as long as possible, up to 24 hours.
2. Preheat the grill to its highest setting, or get a griddle pan really hot.
3. Toss the salad in the salad dressing.
4. Season the lamb steaks with a little salt. Grill or griddle them, turning once, until both sides are a good brown colour.
5. Slice the steaks into thin strips.
6. Open the pitta breads lengthways and toast or grill until warm. Half fill the pitta breads with the salad, then divide the lamb slices between them. Serve with chilli dipping sauce or soured cream handed out separately if required.

LAMB AND CHICKPEA CURRY

This curry is incredibly easy to make. Choose a ready-made curry paste to suit your palate; a Korma is very mild while Madras and Vindaloo curry pastes will give a spicy kick. The chickpeas add texture and fibre and make the dish more economical. Serve the curry with hot boiled basmati rice and a green salad.

All curries benefit from being made a day or two in advance and then stored in the refridgerator. This dish can be frozen for up to three months.

Preparation time: 20 minutes
Cooking time: 1 hour
Serves 4

*675g/1½lb trimmed lamb, cut
    into 5cm/2in cubes*
½ teaspoon salt
2 tablespoons curry paste
2 tablespoons oil
1 large onion, finely chopped
2 cloves garlic, crushed

*1 × 400g/14oz can chopped
    tomatoes in juice*
*1 × 400g/14oz can chickpeas,
    drained and rinsed*

To serve
4 tablespoons Greek yoghurt
*2 tablespoons chopped fresh
    coriander*

1. Toss the lamb with the salt and the curry paste and set aside.
2. Place the oil in a saucepan and stir in the onion. Cover with a damp piece of greaseproof paper, put a lid on the pan and cook over low heat until soft. Remove the lid and paper, increase the heat to a medium setting and cook the onions until they are golden brown in colour.
3. Stir in the garlic and cook for 1 minute.
4. Add the lamb and cook, stirring, for 2–3 minutes. The spices should be cooked but do not allow them to burn.
5. Add the tomatoes and juice and the chickpeas to the pan. Simmer, then cover with a lid and cook until the meat is tender, about 1 hour.
6. Serve topped with the yoghurt and the fresh coriander.

THYME-WRAPPED LAMB

Supermarkets now sell well-trimmed pieces of best end of neck fillet –
they are relatively expensive but there is no wastage at all. This recipe
makes a really simple but sophisticated dinner-party dish. It is best
prepared a day in advance and then cooked at the last minute. Serve
with small roast potatoes and a selection of vegetables.

Preparation time: 20 minutes (plus at least 1 hour resting time)
Cooking time: 15 minutes
Serves 4

2 *pieces of best end neck fillet,* *well trimmed*	*salt and freshly ground black* *pepper*
12 *rashers rindless streaky* *bacon*	2 *tablespoons oil*
3 *tablespoons finely chopped* *fresh thyme*	To serve *redcurrant jelly*

1. Trim any fat and membrane from the lamb fillets. Season with salt and
pepper and rub the thyme over the meat until evenly covered.
2. Lay out 6 rashers of bacon on a piece of clingfilm, just touching each
other. Cover with another piece of clingfilm and roll firmly with a rolling
pin until the rashers join together and form 1 thin, even sheet of bacon.
3. Remove the top sheet of clingfilm and roll 1 fillet in the bacon so that the
rashers wrap around the circumference of the lamb leaving a 2.5cm/1in
overlap.
4. Roll tightly in a long piece of clingfilm, and twist and knot the ends to
keep the roll secure. Repeat with the other fillet. Refrigerate for at least 1
hour or overnight.
5. Preheat the oven to 240°C/430°F/gas mark 8.
6. Remove the clingfilm from the lamb fillets. Heat the oil in a frying pan
and brown the fillets, frying the bacon joins first to seal the rolls. When
evenly browned, remove from the pan and cool on a wire rack until
required.
7. Roast the lamb for 10–12 minutes at the top of the oven until medium-
rare. Rest the lamb for 5 minutes.
8. Slice the lamb on the diagonal into 5–6 slices per fillet. Serve with the
redcurrant jelly.

BLUE-CHEESE BURGERS

These are not really burgers – they are flat meatballs filled with blue cheeses – but they look like burgers, and taste like them until you come across the wonderfully rich cheesy centres. The recipe suggests frying the burgers, but if preferred they can be grilled for 3–4 minutes each side. Serve with a green salad and some chutney.

Preparation time: 30 minutes
Cooking time: 10 minutes
Serves 4

85g/3oz Cambazola cheese
85g/3oz Stilton cheese
450g/1lb very lean minced
  beef
30g/1oz flat-leaf parsley, finely
  chopped
1 egg, beaten

salt and freshly ground black
  pepper
4 soft white rolls, warmed
oil for frying

To serve
green salad

1. In a small bowl, mash the Cambazola with a fork until creamy. Crumble the Stilton into the bowl and mix the cheeses together. Divide into 4 portions and chill.
2. Put the minced beef, parsley and beaten egg into a large bowl and season well with salt and black pepper. Mix together thoroughly.
3. Divide the beef mixture into four equal portions and roll each piece into a ball. Using your thumb, make a deep well in the centre of each ball and push a quarter of the cheese mixture inside. Cover with the meat to seal completely, and flatten the burgers slightly with the palm of your hand. Chill for 20 minutes.
4. Heat a little oil in a heavy-based frying pan and brown the cheese burgers on both sides. Reduce the heat and continue to cook for a further 3–4 minutes on each side.
5. Serve between heated, halved soft rolls.

STEAK WITH MUSHROOMS IN SAGE BUTTER

This is a variation on the classic steak and mushrooms. The portobello mushrooms have an excellent meaty texture. A fillet steak will take a little longer to cook than sirloin steak; it is very much closer in texture. Serve with plenty of mashed potatoes and green vegetables.

Preparation time: 10 minutes
Cooking time: 5 minutes
Serves 4

85g/3oz unsalted butter
8 portobello mushrooms,
  quartered
12 large sage leaves, very finely
  chopped
salt and freshly ground black pepper

1 teaspoon lemon juice
1 tablespoon creamed horseradish
4 × 170g/6oz fillet or sirloin
  steaks
oil for frying

1. Melt the butter in a large frying pan and fry the mushrooms briskly for 1–2 minutes or until well browned.
2. Reduce the heat, stir in the chopped sage and season with salt and black pepper. Reduce the heat and continue to cook very slowly for 2–3 minutes. Stir in the lemon juice and horseradish.
3. Season the steaks on both sides with salt and black pepper. Heat the oil and when very hot brown the steaks on both sides. Reduce the heat and cook for 2–3 minutes.
4. To serve, put a steak on each of 4 serving plates and pour the mushrooms and sage butter over the top of each steak. Serve immediately.

STEAK STROGANOFF

The classic combination of steak, mushrooms and cream is guaranteed to elicit sighs of delight. This dish can be put together quickly for a dinner party or a special treat.

Chestnut, button or wild mushrooms are all suitable for this recipe. For an extra-quick cooking time, use the 1cm/½in-thick sirloin steaks that are readily available in most supermarkets. For a professional finish, the steaks can be cooked in a griddle pan. The steaks can be marinated for up to 24 hours in advance. However, it is best to leave the cooking until just before serving. Serve with new or jacket potatoes and a green vegetable.

Preparation time: 20 minutes
Cooking time: 20 minutes
Serves 4

4 × 1cm/½in-thick sirloin steaks
salt and freshly ground black
  pepper
1 tablespoon Worcester sauce
2 tablespoons olive oil
1 clove garlic, crushed
45g/1½oz butter
2 tablespoons water

200ml/7oz crème fraîche
1 teaspoon dry English mustard
  powder
1 teaspoon cornflour
200g/7oz mushrooms, thinly
  sliced
1 tablespoon chopped fresh
  parsley

1. Trim the steaks of fat and gristle as necessary. Season lightly with salt and black pepper.
2. For the marinade, place the Worcester sauce, oil and garlic in a shallow dish large enough to hold the steaks in a single layer. Place the steaks in the dish, turning them to coat them in the marinade. Cover the dish with clingfilm and refrigerate until required.
3. Mix together the crème fraîche, mustard and cornflour. Set aside.
4. Heat 15g/½oz of the butter in a frying pan or use to grease a griddle pan. Heat the pan over medium-high heat until it is very hot and just starting to smoke.
5. Remove the steaks from the marinade and place in a single layer in the pan. If necessary this can be done in batches. Cook each steak for 1 minute per side for medium-rare meat. Thicker steaks will need longer cooking time. Watch for the juices to bead on the surface of the steaks before

turning them over.

6. Place the steaks on to a serving dish and cover with foil to keep warm.

7. Tip the water into the hot pan and scrape the bottom to remove the browned juices. Stir the juices into the crème fraîche.

8. In a frying pan over medium heat, melt the remaining butter. Cook the mushrooms until they have yielded their juices and the juices have nearly evaporated.

9. Stir in the crème fraîche mixture and allow to bubble for 1 minute. Taste and season. If the sauce is too thick, add a little water. Pour the sauce over the steaks and serve immediately garnished with the parsley.

CHINESE-STYLE BEEF SALAD

This salad can be prepared in advance – indeed, the beef should be marinated overnight – but it should then be cooked right at the last minute. The recipe calls for 300g of beef but carnivores may prefer to use more – in which case it should be stir-fried in 2 batches.

Preparation time: 25 minutes
Cooking time: 10 minutes
Serves 4–6

300g/11oz sirloin steak, sliced thinly
2 tablespoons oil
1 pack baby corn, thinly sliced on
   the diagonal
1 head bok choy, shredded
½ can water chestnuts, sliced
1 bunch spring onions, sliced on
   the diagonal
110g/4oz mangetout, sliced on
   the diagonal
½ bag beansprouts

For the marinade
100ml/3½ fl oz dark soy sauce
55ml/2fl oz sherry
2.5cm/1in ginger, bruised
2 cloves garlic, crushed
2 red chillis, sliced
2 tablespoons honey

To serve
1 × 250g/9oz cooked noodles

1. Mix together the marinade ingredients, add the beef and marinate overnight.

2. Remove the beef from the marinade and pat very lightly with kitchen paper. Strain and reserve the marinade.

3. Heat the oil in a wok, add the beef and stir-fry for 1 minute. Using a

slotted spoon, remove the beef from the frying pan and keep warm.
4. Meanwhile, cook the noodles as per the manufacturer's instructions.
5. Add the corn, water chestnuts, spring onions and bok choy to the wok and stir-fry together for 2 minutes. Add the mangetout and beansprouts and cook for a further 2 minutes. Remove the vegetables from the pan and keep warm.
6. Add the marinade to the wok and boil rapidly until it has reduced to half its original quantity. Return the beef and vegetables to the wok, reheat and serve with the noodles.

THAI-STYLE BURGERS

The curry pastes now available in the supermarkets are markedly superior to those even 3 or 4 years ago. Use more or less paste according to taste. These burgers can be made in advance but should be cooked at the last minute. They can be served in baps or even with noodles or rice.

Preparation time: 20 minutes
Cooking time: 6–10 minutes
Serves 4

1 tablespoon sunflower oil
1 medium red onion, chopped
1 tablespoon Thai green curry paste
1 red chilli, finely chopped
3 tablespoons freshly chopped coriander
4 spring onions, finely chopped

450g/1lb lean beef, minced
salt and pepper

To serve
soured cream mixed with freshly chopped coriander and the zest of 1 lime
sweet chilli sauce

1. Heat the oil in a heavy-based saucepan, add the onion and cook slowly until soft. Add the curry paste and fry for 30–45 seconds. Remove from the heat and allow to cool.
2. In a large bowl, combine the cooled cooked onions with the remaining ingredients. Season well with salt and pepper.
3. Make the hamburgers: with wet hands, shape the meat into flattish rounds of equal size and make a slight dip in the centre of each one. The burgers will shrink and thicken when they cook.
4. Grill steadily, turning once. Allow 3 minutes each side for rare burgers,

or 5 minutes each side for well done.

5. Serve in a bap or pitta bread with the soured-cream mixture and sweet chilli sauce.

LEMON CHICKEN

This is a quick supper dish that can be made at the last minute. Let the frying pan cool for a couple of minutes before adding the lemon juice – it burns very easily. Serve with pasta or mashed potatoes and a green vegetable.

Preparation time: 10 minutes
Cooking time: 10 minutes
Serves 4

4 × 170g/6oz chicken breasts,
* skinned and boned*
juice and zest of 1 lemon
1 tablespoon oil
30g/1oz butter
3 tablespoons dry vermouth

caster sugar
salt and freshly ground black
* pepper*

To serve
sprigs of watercress

1. Slice the chicken breasts finely on the horizontal.

2. Sprinkle the lemon zest over the chicken breasts.

3. Heat the oil in a large frying pan, add half the butter and quickly fry the breasts until brown on both sides and just cooked (it may be necessary to do this in 2 batches).

4. Keep the chicken warm while you make the sauce. Add the lemon juice, remaining butter and the vermouth to the pan and bring to the boil. Stir well and simmer for 1 minute. Add sugar, salt and pepper to taste.
5. To serve, pour the sauce over the chicken and garnish with sprigs of watercress.

TURKEY STEAKS WITH GINGER AND TOMATO SALSA

Turkey steaks are now available in most supermarkets. They are very low in fat, taste delicious and can be cooked in 4 minutes. The salsa can be made a day in advance – the flavours will develop overnight. If lemon oil is not available use olive oil and add the grated zest of a lemon or lime.

Preparation time: 20 minutes
Cooking time: 6 minutes
Serves 6

6 turkey steaks
2 tablespoons oil
30g/1oz butter

For the salsa
1 red pepper
2 small red onions, finely
  chopped
3 tablespoons lemon olive oil
2 tomatoes, peeled, deseeded and
  finely chopped

1 × 2½cm/1in piece ginger,
  peeled and finely chopped
1 tablespoon coriander, roughly
  chopped
salt and freshly ground black
  pepper

To serve
fresh coriander leaves

1. Cut the pepper into quarters, remove the membrane and seeds. Grill the skin side of the peppers until blistered and blackened all over. Allow to cool, then remove the skin. Finely chop the pepper flesh.
2. Mix together the chopped peppers and the remaining salsa ingredients.
3. Heat the oil in a large frying pan, add the butter and fry the turkey steaks for 2–3 minutes per side.
4. Arrange the turkey on a serving plate, garnish with the fresh coriander leaves and hand out the salsa separately.

BAKED STUFFED CHICKEN BREASTS WITH SUNDRIED TOMATOES, SAGE AND PARMA HAM

This is a simple chicken dish that can be prepared in advance and refrigerated until required. Baste the chicken with the cooking juices a couple of times to improve the flavour. It is important that the breast is neither overcooked nor kept warm for any length of time; in either case it will become dry and tough.

Preparation time: 20 minutes
Cooking time: 30 minutes
Serves 4

2 slices Parma ham
3 sundried tomatoes in olive oil, drained
8 large sage leaves
1 tablespoon Parmesan cheese, freshly grated
2 tablespoons sundried tomato oil from the jar

4 chicken breasts, boned
100ml/3½fl oz dry white wine or vermouth

To garnish
watercress

1. Preheat the oven to 200°C/400°F/gas mark 6.
2. Shred the Parma ham, and finely chop the sundried tomatoes and sage.
3. Mix together with the grated Parmesan, salt and freshly ground black pepper and ½ a tablespoon of the sundried tomato oil.
4. Divide the mixture evenly between the 4 chicken breasts: push the mixture under the skin of each breast, smoothing the skin over the stuffing to secure it.
5. Put the stuffed chicken breasts into a roasting pan and season the skin with salt and black pepper. Pour the remaining oil over the chicken and bake on the top shelf of the preheated oven for 25–35 minutes. Pour the white wine or vermouth over the chicken and cook for a further 5 minutes, or until the chicken juices run clear when the meat pierced with a skewer and the skin is brown and crisp.
6. Serve the chicken with the pan juices poured over it. Garnish with sprigs of watercress.

SMOKED CHICKEN SALAD WITH BLACK PUDDING

This is a seriously hearty first course that can alternatively be served as a main course. The recipe calls for a soft-boiled egg, in other words an egg that has been boiled for about 8 minutes – the yolk should be almost but not quite set. The dressing is quite thick, so you might find that you do not need it all.

Preparation time: 20 minutes
Cooking time: 10 minutes
Serves 4

4 slices black pudding
1 bag bistro salad
55g/2oz cherry tomatoes, quartered
2 smoked chicken breasts, cut into thin slices
2 soft-boiled eggs, shelled and halved

For the dressing
1 tablespoon balsamic vinegar
3 tablespoons good-quality olive oil
1 teaspoon grainy mustard
salt and freshly ground black pepper

1. Make the dressing: mix together all the ingredients.
2. Fry the black pudding in a heavy-based frying pan until crisp on both sides.
3. Mix together the salad leaves and tomatoes and toss in half the dressing.
4. Divide the salad between 4 large plates, Arrange the smoked chicken slices on top.
5. Place the black pudding on top of the chicken and the soft-boiled egg halves on the top of that.
6. Drizzle a little more of the dressing over each portion and serve immediately.

CHICKEN BIRYANI

This is a simplified version of chicken biryani. The number of ingredients may look daunting but all you have to do to make the sauce is whizz everything together in a food processor until smooth. If you have time, garnish the finished sauce with raisins and cashew nuts which have been fried in butter.

Preparation time: 15 minutes
Cooking time: 35 minutes
Serves 4

4 chicken breasts, skinned, boned and cut into cubes
2 tablespoons oil
30g/1oz butter, or ghee if available
1 onion, chopped
285g/10oz basmati rice, washed and drained
500ml/18fl oz chicken stock or water
5 strands saffron soaked in 2 tablespoons hot water

For the sauce
1 teaspoon ground cinnamon
½ teaspoon each of ground cumin, coriander, paprika, cardamom, turmeric and cloves
2 green chillis, roughly chopped
1 onion, roughly chopped
5 cloves garlic, peeled
30g/1oz coriander leaves
5cm/2in piece fresh ginger, peeled and finely chopped
1 tablespoon tomato purée
salt
225g/8fl oz plain yoghurt

1. Preheat the oven to 170°C/325°F/gas mark 3.
2. In a food processor or blender, mix together all the ingredients for the sauce until smooth.
3. In a large frying pan, heat half of the oil and butter/ghee. Fry the chicken pieces until lightly browned all over. Add the sauce ingredients, bring to the boil and then simmer until the chicken is tender.
4. Meanwhile, melt the remaining oil and butter/ghee, add the onion and cook for 5 minutes or until golden brown. Add the rice and fry for a further 5 minutes or until translucent. Add the stock, and season with salt and pepper. Bring to the boil and cook until just tender – about 10 minutes. Drain well.
5. In a lightly greased casserole dish, layer the rice and chicken together, finishing with a layer of rice. Pour the saffron in its water over the top of the biryani, cover tightly and bake for 15 minutes.

CHICKEN TERIYAKI

Teriyaki is a Japanese dish for which the meat is marinated in soy sauce, sugar and seasonings before cooking. It is a great marinade for meat cooked on a barbecue – but if weather is not permitting, the dish can be cooked in the oven with equally delicious results. If you wish to use your marinade as a sauce for the cooked meat, it must be boiled for 5 minutes.

The recipe uses dark soy sauce, which is less salty than the regular soy sauce and is perfect for marinades, but regular soy sauce can be used instead. The meat can be marinated for up to 24 hours if stored in the refrigerator, but if time is short the recipe works well if the marinade is poured over the meat just prior to baking.

Serve the teriyaki with boiled rice and stir-fried vegetables or salad.

Preparation time: 10 minutes
Cooking time: 55 minutes
Serves 4

8 boneless, skinless chicken thighs
100ml/3½fl oz dark soy sauce
100ml/3½fl oz rice wine or dry
   white wine
2 tablespoons sesame oil or
   sunflower oil
2 tablespoons caster sugar
2 tablespoons runny honey
1 clove garlic, crushed
1 tablespoon grated fresh ginger
1–2 teaspoons cornflour
6 spring onions, cut into 5cm/2in
   lengths

1. Place the chicken thighs in a single layer in an ovenproof dish.
2. In a small bowl, combine the remaining ingredients except the cornflour and spring onions. Pour the mixture over the chicken. Turn the chicken in the marinade to coat, then cover with tinfoil. Refrigerate until ready to cook.
3. Preheat the oven to 200°C/400°F/gas mark 6 or light the barbecue.
4. Bake the chicken for 30 minutes, basting once after 15 minutes. Remove the tinfoil and cook for a further 10 minutes. Ensure that the chicken is cooked all the way through: the juices should run clear when the meat is cut at its thickest part.
5. Transfer the chicken from the baking dish to a serving dish and cover with tinfoil to keep warm.
6. Sieve the pan juices (or the marinade if cooking on the barbecue) into a large saucepan. Mix the cornflour with 1 tablespoon of water. Stir into the sauce, then boil until syrupy, about 5 minutes.
7. Add the spring onion to the sauce and pour over the chicken to serve.

TURKEY GOUJONS WITH SWEET AND SOUR SAUCE

Turkey escalopes are widely available in supermarkets – they have a good flavour and are very versatile. This recipe is particularly popular with children. If preferred, the goujons can be fried in shallow fat for 2–3 minutes.

Preparation time: 15 minutes
Cooking time: 15 minutes
Serves 4

4 small turkey breast escalopes
4 tablespoons seasoned flour plus
  ¼ teaspoon chilli powder
2 eggs, beaten
55g/2oz dried white breadcrumbs

For the sauce
1 teaspoon cornflour
4 tablespoons water

2 tablespoons sugar
2 tablespoons wine vinegar
2 tablespoons tomato purée
2 tablespoons orange juice
2 tablespoons soy sauce
lemon juice to taste
oil for frying

1. Cut the turkey escalopes into slices approximately 1.5cm/⅝in wide. Dip the slices into the flour and pat off the excess, cover in the beaten egg and finally in the breadcrumbs. Ensure that the goujons are completely covered, then lay them in a single layer on a large plate and refrigerate.
2. Make the sauce: blend the cornflour with the water and then mix in the sugar, vinegar, tomato purée, orange juice and soy sauce. Transfer to a small pan and heat gently until boiling, then simmer for 1 minute. If the sauce is too thick, add more water. Adjust to taste if necessary with either sugar or lemon juice.
3. Heat the oil in a deep-fat fryer until a crumb will sizzle in it.
4. Fry a few goujons at a time until crisp and golden brown. Drain well on absorbent paper and sprinkle with salt.
5. Serve immediately with the sweet and sour sauce.

CHICKEN AND MUSHROOM PIES

These chicken pies are ideal for using up any leftover cooked chicken. They can be made a day in advance and then baked when required. Serve with a green salad.

Preparation time: 25 minutes
Cooking time 40 minutes
Serves 4

For the filling
45g/1½ tablespoons butter
3 shallots, very finely chopped
170g/6oz button mushrooms, stalks removed and quartered
45g/1½oz plain flour
425ml/¾ pint milk
2 teaspoons finely chopped sage
salt and freshly ground black pepper

450g/1lb cooked chicken, cut into large pieces

For the topping
2 × 140g/5oz vermicelli nests
2 slices Parma ham, roughly chopped
2 teaspoons finely chopped sage
20g/¾oz butter, melted

1. Make the filling: melt the butter in a saucepan, add the shallots and cook over a gentle heat until softened but not coloured.
2. Add the mushrooms to the pan and increase the heat. Cook briskly for 3–4 minutes or until nicely browned. Stir in the flour and cook for a further minute.
3. Reduce the heat and slowly add the milk. Bring to the boil and simmer for 1 minute. Stir in the sage and season with salt and pepper. Allow to cool.
4. Meanwhile, make the topping: cook the vermicelli according to the packet instructions. Drain. Stir in the Parma ham and sage and season with salt and pepper.
5. Preheat the oven to 200°C/400°F/gas mark 6.
6. Stir the chicken into the cooked mushroom sauce and mix well. Divide the mixture between 4 individual ovenproof serving dishes.
7. Loosely pile the vermicelli on top of each dish and place on to a baking sheet. Brush with the melted butter and bake in the centre of the oven for 20–25 minutes or until the pies are hot and bubbling and the vermicelli is crisp and brown.

BALTI CHICKEN

Balti curries from northern Pakistan are easy-to-make, one-dish meals. Use Balti curry paste for spice and flavour, then choose a combination of meat, vegetables and pulses; serve with basmati rice if desired.

Preparation time: 10 minutes
Cooking time: 15–20 minutes
Serves 4

1 onion, chopped
4 tablespoons vegetable oil
110g/4oz new potatoes, cut into 1cm/½in cubes
2 small green peppers, cut into 2cm/¾in cubes
1 × 400g/14oz can chopped tomatoes

450g/1lb boneless, skinless chicken breast cut into bite-sized pieces
4 tablespoons Balti curry paste

To serve
2 tablespoons chopped fresh coriander
4 tablespoons thick natural yoghurt

1. Fry the onion in half the oil until it starts to soften, about 10 minutes.
2. Add the potato and green pepper and fry to brown lightly.
3. Place the vegetables in a saucepan. Add the tomatoes and simmer.
4. Season the chicken and brown lightly in the remaining oil.
5. Stir in the Balti paste and cook for 30 seconds. Add 2 tablespoons of water, then add the chicken and spices to the vegetables.
6. Simmer until the chicken and vegetables are cooked through, about 15 minutes. Serve garnished with coriander and yoghurt.

PEANUT CHICKEN

This chicken makes an ideal family supper dish. It can be completely prepared a day in advance, and in fact improves the longer the chicken is left in the marinade. While the chicken is baking, some of the stuffing will probably fall out; don't worry – this can be incorporated into the pan juices at the end. Simply skim off any fat and reduce the juices to a syrupy consistency. Use any Chinese-style cooking sauce that appeals. We use one containing garlic, chilli, soy and honey.

Preparation time: 10 minutes (excluding marinating time)
Cooking time: 25 minutes
Serves 4

8 boned chicken thighs
1 × 200ml/6fl oz jar good-quality Chinese-style cooking sauce

For the stuffing
1 tablespoon oil
2 spring onions, finely chopped
1 red chilli, finely chopped
4 tablespoons crunchy peanut butter

½ tablespoon coriander, freshly chopped
1 tablespoon dark soy sauce
1 tablespoon lemon juice

To serve
egg noodles
soy sauce
30g/1oz dry-roasted peanuts, chopped

1. In a heavy-based frying pan or wok, heat the oil and cook the spring onions and red chilli for 1–2 minutes. Remove from the pan and mix together with the other stuffing ingredients.
2. Divide the stuffing between the chicken thighs where the bones have been removed. Secure the edges together on each one with a cocktail stick.
3. Place the chicken thighs in a shallow dish. Pour over the cooking sauce. Leave the chicken to marinate overnight or for as long as possible.
4. Preheat the oven to 200°C/400°F/gas mark 6.
5. Remove the chicken from the marinade and place skin-side up in a shallow roasting tin and bake in the preheated oven for 25 minutes.
6. Remove from the oven when the skin is golden brown and the chicken is cooked.
7. Remove the cocktail sticks and serve immediately on a bed of egg noodles which have been tossed in soy sauce. Sprinkle with the chopped peanuts.

SAUSAGES WITH RED ONION AND PORT SAUCE

This is a variation on the classic theme of sausages with onion gravy. The addition of port and thyme lends a certain element of sophistication. This dish is particularly good with mashed potatoes to which a tablespoon of grainy mustard has been added.

Preparation time: 5 minutes
Cooking time: 25 minutes
Serves 4

8–12 good-quality sausages
1 tablespoon sunflower oil
2 red onions, finely sliced
1 heaped teaspoon plain flour
5 tablespoons port

150ml/¼ pint stock
1 teaspoon fresh thyme, finely
  chopped
salt and freshly ground black
  pepper

1. Preheat the oven to 180°C/350°F/gas mark 4.
2. Heat the oil in a large frying pan. Fry the sausages over a moderate heat until lightly browned. Remove the pan from the heat and transfer the sausages to a baking sheet. Finish cooking them in the preheated oven for 20–30 minutes.
3. Remove the excess oil from the frying pan, add the onions and cook until soft and golden brown.
4. Add the flour to the pan and cook, stirring, for 1 minute.
5. Slowly add the port and stock to the pan, bring to the boil and simmer for 3 minutes. Add the thyme, and season to taste with salt and pepper. Serve with the sausages and mustard mashed potato.

SAUSAGES AND PARSNIPS WITH HONEY AND MUSTARD

This dish can be prepared in advance and then baked an hour before you are ready to serve. These sausages make ideal comfort food. Serve with mashed potatoes and a green salad.

Preparation time: 35 minutes
Cooking time: 1 hour
Serves 4

8 good-quality pork sausages
450g/1lb parsnips, peeled and cut
  into small wedges
3 onions, peeled and cut into
  eighths
675g/1½lb soft mashed potato

2 tablespoons freshly chopped
  flat-leaf parsley
salt and freshly ground black
  pepper
1½ tablespoons runny honey
1½ tablespoons grainy mustard
2 teaspoons English mustard

1. Preheat the oven to 190°C/375°F/gas mark 5.
2. Prick the sausages and place them in a large roasting tin in the oven for
10 minutes or until the fat is beginning to run from them. Add the parsnips
and onions and toss together in the fat. If the sausages are very lean and no
fat has been released, add a little sunflower oil.
3. Continue to roast the sausages and vegetables for another 45 minutes,
turning them every so often so that they brown on all sides.
4. Meanwhile, make the mashed potato, season with salt and black pepper
and stir in the parsley.
5. Mix together the honey and mustards. Pour the mixture over the
sausages and vegetables and stir through. Return to the oven for another 10
minutes.
6. Serve the sausages and vegetables with the mashed potato immediately.

PORK MEDALLIONS WITH MUSTARD SAUCE

This simple dish is great for autumn evenings: mashed potato soaks up
the sauce and turns it into perfect comfort food. Crème fraîche is an
ideal ingredient for making pan sauces because it can be boiled
without curdling and gives a delightfully smooth finish.

Preparation time: 5 minutes
Cooking time: 10 minutes
Serves 4

675g/1½lb pork fillet
salt and freshly ground black pepper
30g/1oz unsalted butter
3 tablespoons water
150ml/¼ pint crème fraîche
2 tablespoons Dijon mustard

To serve
mashed potato
green vegetables

To garnish
chopped fresh parsley

1. Trim the pork fillet of any fat and membrane. Cut into slices 2.5cm/1in thick. Flatten each slice lightly between clingfilm to approximately half the original thickness.
2. Season the pork with the salt and freshly ground black pepper. Heat the butter in a large frying pan until foaming. Add the pork slices to the pan (in batches if necessary) and cook for 2 minutes on each side until the slices are browned and cooked through. Remove from the pan and keep warm.
3. Add the water to the pan and bring to the boil, continuously scraping the bottom of the pan to remove any sediment. Add the crème fraîche and mustard to the pan and heat through. Taste and season with salt and pepper if necessary.
4. Arrange the pork slices on a plate and pour the sauce over the top. Garnish with the parsley and serve immediately with mashed potato and a green vegetable.

POT-ROAST LOIN OF PORK

A pot-roast is a comforting winter dish, perfect for a Sunday lunch. Ask the butcher to remove the chine bone and the skin from the joint. Serve with baked potatoes and a green vegetable.

Preparation time: 15 minutes
Cooking time: 1 hour 30 minutes
Serves 4–6

2kg/4.5lb loin of pork (skin, most
  of fat and chine bone removed)
2 cloves garlic, peeled and thinly
  sliced
2 tablespoons oil
225g/8oz shallots, peeled
salt and freshly ground black pepper

290ml/½ pint fruity red wine
570ml/1 pint chicken or vegetable
  stock
2 tablespoons chopped fresh
  rosemary
450g/1lb carrots, peeled and cut
  into large chunks

1. Make small slits in the meat and insert the garlic slivers.
2. Heat the oil in a large ovenproof casserole dish over a medium heat. Brown the shallots, then set aside.
3. Preheat the oven to 160°C/325°F/gas mark 3.
4. Season the pork, then brown on all sides. Remove from the pan.
5. Add the wine to the hot pan and bring to the boil. Reduce by boiling rapidly to half its original quantity. Return the pork to the pan with the stock, shallots and rosemary. Bring to the boil. Season with salt and pepper.
6. Cover the casserole with a tight-fitting lid and cook for 1 hour. Add the carrots to the dish and return to the oven for a further 30 minutes.
7. Remove the pork and slice into 1cm/1½in slices. Arrange on a serving dish and surround with the vegetables. Keep warm.
8. Boil the juices to thicken slightly, pour over the pork and serve.

PORK AND GREEN OLIVE BURGERS IN CIABATTA WITH ROAST PEPPERS

These delicious burgers can be made in advance and then frozen or grilled as required. Take great care when chopping chillies – we recommend wearing gloves or using a knife and fork. Deseed the chillies under cold running water.

Preparation time: 15 minutes
Cooking time: 30 minutes
Serves 4

450g/1lb minced pork
85g/3oz green olives, pitted and
   roughly chopped
1 clove garlic, crushed
5 tablespoons fresh coriander,
   roughly chopped
½ red chilli, finely chopped
1 egg, beaten
salt and freshly ground black
   pepper

2 red peppers, deseeded and
   quartered
2 yellow peppers, deseeded and
   quartered
balsamic vinegar
olive oil
4 × ciabatta rolls, or 1 large loaf
   cut into 4

To serve
crisp green salad

117

1. Preheat the grill to its highest setting.

2. Make the pork burgers: mix together the pork, olive, garlic, coriander and chilli. Use as much of the egg as necessary to bind the mixture together, season heavily with salt and pepper and shape the mixture into 4 burgers. Chill until required.

3. Grill the peppers skin-side up until the skin begins to blacken. When cool enough to handle, peel off the skins, drizzle the peppers with balsamic vinegar, salt and pepper and set aside.

4. Brush the burgers with olive oil and grill on both sides until golden brown, then reduce the heat and continue grilling until they are completely cooked through. This will take about 8 minutes.

5. Split the ciabatta and warm through. Assemble the burgers with the peppers and a little of the salad in the ciabatta, and serve with the remaining green salad tossed in 2 tablespoons of olive oil, 2 tablespoons of balsamic vinegar and a little salt and pepper.

SLOW-COOKED PORK BELLY WITH TOMATOES AND THYME

This is perfect comfort cooking, ideal served with plenty of mashed potatoes for a winter supper. It can be made in advance and then reheated or frozen as required. Pork belly is a fairly fatty cut of meat but it becomes beautifully tender once cooked.

Preparation time: 10 minutes
Cooking time: 2 hours
Serves 4

900g/2lb pork belly, off the bone
  and skinned, cut into 2.5cm/1in
  pieces
2 tablespoons olive oil
2 onions, chopped
1 head celery, sliced
2 cloves garlic, crushed
425ml/¾ pint chicken stock

1 × 400g/14oz can plum
  tomatoes
1 bay leaf
1 bunch of thyme

To serve
mashed potatoes

1. Trim the pork belly of most of its fat.

2. Heat 1 tablespoon of the olive oil in a heavy-based saucepan. Add the onion and celery and cook on a medium heat until lightly coloured. Add the garlic and cook for a further minute. Pile on to a plate.

3. Heat the remaining oil in the saucepan and lightly brown the pork pieces, a few at a time. Return the onion, celery and garlic to the pan. Add the chicken stock and tomatoes and season with salt and pepper. Stir well and bring gradually to the boil. Add the bay leaf and thyme and simmer slowly for 1½–2 hours or until tender. Serve with mashed potatoes.

ROAST LOIN OF PORK WITH HONEY AND KUMQUAT GLAZE

The acidity of the kumquat glaze balances the richness of the pork beautifully. This is ideal for a dinner party – the pork can be kept warm for 10–15 minutes. Serve with mashed potatoes and a green vegetable.

Preparation time: 15 minutes
Cooking time: 1 hour 40 minutes
Serves 4

85g/3oz kumquats
1 tablespoon clear honey
110g/4oz soft light brown sugar
2 teaspoons English mustard
1.13kg/2½lb loin of pork, on the
  bone, chined and skin removed
5 tablespoons water

For the sauce
290ml/½ pint chicken stock
15g/½oz cornflour (optional)
1 tablespoon white wine vinegar
salt and freshly ground black
  pepper

1. Preheat the oven to 200°C/400°F/gas mark 6.

2. Cover the kumquats with cold water in a saucepan and bring to the boil. Then lower the heat and simmer for 3 minutes. Drain and return the kumquats to the pan.

3. Put the honey, sugar and mustard into the saucepan. Stir well and allow the sugar to dissolve. Boil very briefly until the kumquats are lightly glazed.

4. Place the pork, fatty-side up, in a roasting tin. Add the water.

5. With a sharp knife, score the pork fat in a lattice pattern. Spoon the glaze over the meat, leaving the kumquats in the bottom of the saucepan. Roast the pork in the preheated oven for 1½ hours. Keep warm in the turned-off oven.

6. Make the sauce: add the stock to the roasting tin. Bring gradually to the boil, stirring well to collect any sediment from the bottom of the tin. Taste and reduce, by boiling, to a syrupy consistency. Mix the cornflour with 2 tablespoons of water. Add to the gravy and boil briefly. Add the vinegar and reserved kumquats and season to taste with salt and pepper.

7. Spoon a little of the sauce and as many of the kumquats as possible over the pork and hand out the remainder in a warmed sauceboat.

GAMMON STEAKS WITH MUSTARD AND BITTER-ORANGE GLAZE

Gammon steaks are readily available in most supermarkets. If they come with a lot of fat and rind, cut off the rind and snip the fat at regular intervals. This will prevent it from curling up when grilled.

Preparation time: 10 minutes
Cooking time: 6 minutes
Serves 4

*4 × 170g/6oz thick-cut gammon
  steaks*
freshly ground black pepper
*3 tablespoons dark orange
  marmalade, chopped*

*2 teaspoons soft light brown
  sugar*
*½ tablespoon wholegrain
  mustard*
¼ teaspoon mixed spice

1. Preheat the grill to its highest setting.

2. Season the gammon steaks with black pepper and grill on both sides for 2–3 minutes.

3. Meanwhile, put the marmalade, sugar, mustard and mixed spice into a small saucepan and heat gently, stirring occasionally. Remove the gammon steaks from the heat. Brush with the orange glaze and return to the grill for a further 1–2 minutes or until the glaze is hot and beginning to bubble and caramelise.

4. Serve immediately.

CHORIZO QUESIDILLAS WITH CORIANDER AND CHILLI SALAD

Mexican food is becoming more and more popular and children who don't generally like spicy food seem to enjoy this style. Quesidillas are tortilla snacks that can be stuffed with a variety of Mexican ingredients. Here they are served with a salad as a main course, but they can also be served as a first course with guacamole, tomato salsa or soured cream. Chipotle salsa is made from sundried chillies and has a delicious flavour, but if it is not available use any spicy tomato sauce.

This recipe sounds complicated because it has lots of ingredients, but it requires very little skill to prepare. The sandwiches can be made in advance and then fried at the last minute.

Preparation time: 15 minutes
Cooking time: 10–15 minutes
Serves 4

For the quesidillas
8 soft flour tortillas
4 tablespoons chipotle chilli salsa
110g/4oz strong Cheddar cheese, grated
1 chorizo sausage, finely sliced
3 tablespoons olive oil

For the salad dressing
85g/3oz mayonnaise
½ green chilli, finely chopped
zest and juice of 1 lime

½ small bunch coriander, roughly chopped
salt and freshly ground black pepper

For the salad
110g/4oz can black beans, rinsed and drained
55g/2oz can sweetcorn, drained
1 small iceberg lettuce, torn into bite-size pieces
½ small bunch coriander, leaves only

1. Prepare the salad dressing. In a food processor or blender, mix together all the ingredients until smooth. Season to taste with salt and pepper.
2. Toss all the salad ingredients together.
3. Make the quesidillas: spread each tortilla with a thin layer of the chipotle sauce and then sprinkle 4 of them with grated cheese and the chorizo sausage. Top with the remaining tortillas to make a sandwich.
4. Heat a tablespoon of oil in a heavy-based frying pan and fry the first 'sandwich' on both sides until the cheese has melted and the tortilla is golden brown. Repeat with the other 3 tortillas, adding more oil when necessary.
5. Cut the tortillas into wedges. Toss the salad in the dressing, pile on to plates and top with the quesidillas.

DUCK BREASTS WITH BLACKBERRY AND APPLE SAUCE

Duck breasts are now readily available in most good supermarkets. They are quick and easy to cook but make for an elegant and reasonably priced sophisticated dinner-party dish. When frying the duck a lot of fat will be released, so you may need to drain some of it from the pan so that it does not spit.
  Serve with crushed new potatoes and a green vegetable.

Preparation time: 10 minutes
Cooking time: 10 minutes
Serves 4

4 large duck breasts, skin on	*1½ tablespoons water*
110g/4oz blackberries	*finely grated zest of ½ lemon*
1 small dessert apple, peeled, cored	*sugar to taste*
* and cut into 2cm/¾in chunks*	*salt and pepper*
1 tablespoon port	*oil for frying*

1. Make a lattice pattern on the duck skin and sprinkle with salt.
2. Preheat the oven to 220°C/425°F/gas mark 7.
3. Wash the blackberries and put into a small saucepan with the apples. Add the port, water, lemon zest, and about 15g/½oz caster sugar (less if the blackberries are very ripe) and heat very gently until the fruit begins to soften and the juices are thick and syrupy. Taste, season with black pepper and add more sugar if the sauce is very tart – but don't add too much, as the final sauce should be a little sharp.

4. Heat a small amount of oil in a heavy-based frying pan. When hot, add the duck breast, skin-side down, and fry until the skin becomes a good even brown colour (about the colour of roast chicken). Remove the duck from the frying pan and put skin-side up into a roasting tin.
5. Roast the duck in the preheated oven for 8–10 minutes or until the duck is cooked but still pink.
6. Remove from the oven, cut into slices on the diagonal and serve with the warm blackberry and apple sauce.

THAI-STYLE DUCK AND NOODLE SALAD

This duck salad can be served as a first course or as a main course; these quantities assume that it is for a first course. The recipe calls for fish sauce, which is now readily available in major supermarkets. However, if you can't find it you can use soy sauce instead.

Preparation and cooking time: 25 minutes
Serves 4

2 duck breasts, skin on
125g/4½oz medium-thread egg noodles
100g/3½oz shiitake mushrooms, sliced
1 large handful of fresh coriander
1 red chilli, deseeded and finely diced
zest of 1 lime
1 bunch spring onions, sliced

55g/2oz blanched cashew nuts, toasted
oil for frying

For the dressing
juice of 2 limes
1 tablespoon light soy sauce
1 tablespoon rice wine vinegar
1 tablespoon fish sauce
1 tablespoon honey

1. Preheat the oven to 200°C/400°F/gas mark 6.

2. Trim the duck breasts of any membranes or sinew. Score the skin side in a lattice pattern with a sharp knife and season well with salt and pepper.

3. Heat a heavy-based frying pan and place the duck breasts in it, skin-side down. Fry over a medium heat for 5 minutes, until the skin is well browned. As the duck skin browns it will release a lot of fat which should be tipped out of the frying pan at intervals or the skin will not become crisp.

4. Mix together the dressing ingredients and set aside

5. Roast the duck in the oven for 8–10 minutes; it should remain slightly pink. Allow to rest for 5 minutes.

6. Fry the shiitake mushrooms in a little oil until just soft.

7. Put the mushrooms, coriander, chilli, lime zest, spring onion and cashews into a large bowl.

8. Cook the noodles according to the instructions, drain well and add to the salad ingredients.

9. Pour the dressing over the salad and mix thoroughly.

10. Slice the duck breast on the diagonal. Serve the salad warm, with the duck slices arranged overlapping on the top.

DUCK BREASTS WITH ORANGES

This is a simplified version of the classic duck with orange sauce. The sauce is very quick to make, and it has a sharp, tangy flavour that contrasts well with the rich duck flesh. Serve with plenty of mashed potatoes and peas.

Preparation time: 15 minutes
Cooking time: 25 minutes
Serves 4

4 duck breasts, skin on
salt and freshly ground black
  pepper
1 tablespoon oil
5 tablespoons chicken stock
2 tablespoons sherry vinegar

To serve
mashed potatoes
peas

To garnish
sprigs of chervil
orange segments

1. Preheat the oven to 200°C/400°F/gas mark 6.
2. Make 4–5 diagonal slashes through the duck skin and season with salt and black pepper.
3. Heat the oil in a frying pan and fry the duck breasts skin-side down for 4–5 minutes or until the skin is crisp and brown. Drain off any excess fat.
4. Transfer the duck breasts to a wire rack placed over a roasting tin and bake in the preheated oven for 7–10 minutes or until pink and juicy.
5. Remove the duck breasts and keep warm. Pour off any excess fat and place the pan over direct heat. Add the stock and bring to the boil, scraping the bottom of the pan to remove any sediment. Add the vinegar and simmer until syrupy, skimming off any fat. Season to taste.
6. Slice the duck breasts and serve with orange segments and the pan juices poured over the top. Garnish with sprigs of chervil.

DUCK BREASTS WITH DRIED CHERRY SAUCE

Duck breasts can be fatty, so prior to roasting it is important to fry them skin-side down until they are a good even brown colour. During this time a lot of the duck fat will be released into the frying pan. This frying can be done in advance but if the duck is cold when you are ready to roast it, extend the cooking time to 10–15 minutes.

Preparation time: 10 minutes
Cooking time: 15 minutes
Serves 4

4 large duck breasts, skin on
salt and pepper
oil for frying

For the sauce
30g/1oz butter
1 onion, finely chopped

soft brown sugar
140g/5oz dried cherries (or size of
pack)
290ml/½ pint red wine
salt and freshly ground black
pepper

1. With a knife, make a lattice pattern on the duck skin and sprinkle with salt.
2. Preheat the oven to 220°C/425°F/gas mark 7.
3. Heat a small amount of oil in a heavy-based frying pan. When the oil is hot, add the duck and fry as described above. When the skin looks about

the colour of roast chicken, remove the duck from the frying pan and set aside, skin-side up, on a wire rack over a roasting tin, ready to put in the oven.

4. Make the sauce: melt the butter, add the onions and cook slowly until soft but not coloured. Increase the heat, add a little sugar and allow the onions to caramelise; they should become quite dark brown.

5. Add the cherries and red wine and cook slowly until the liquid is reduced by about a third of its original quantity. Season to taste with salt and pepper. Set aside.

6. Roast the duck in the preheated oven for 8–10 minutes or until the meat is cooked but still pink.

7. Once the duck is cooked, drain the fat from the juices in the roasting tin and add the lean juices to the cherry sauce.

8. Cut the duck breasts into slices on the diagonal and serve with the warm cherry sauce.

DUCK WITH STIR-FRIED VEGETABLES AND NOODLES

Preparation for this recipe should begin a day in advance – the longer the duck is left in the marinade, the better. The breasts have been skinned so that this is a relatively low-fat dish.

Preparation time: 15 minutes
Marinade time: overnight
Cooking time: 20 minutes
Serves 4

8 tablespoons soy sauce
2 tablespoons honey or stem
   ginger syrup if available
ground black pepper
2 red chillis, finely chopped
4 Gressingham duck breasts, skinned
1 tablespoon sesame oil
1 bunch spring onions, finely
   chopped
1 red pepper, deseeded and sliced

1 yellow pepper, deseeded and
   sliced
1 small pack baby sweetcorn, cut
   in half on the diagonal
1 small pack of mangetout
1 pack medium egg noodles
30g/1oz sesame seeds, toasted

To serve
fresh coriander leaves

1. In a shallow dish, mix together the soy sauce, honey, ground black pepper and half of the red chilli. Add the duck breast and coat in the marinade, cover and refrigerate overnight or for as long as possible, turning occasionally.

2. Preheat the oven to 200°C/400°F/gas mark 6.

3. Place the duck breasts with half the marinade in a roasting tin and cook in the preheated oven for 15–20 minutes. Reserve the remaining marinade.

4. Cook the noodles according to the manufacturer's instructions. Meanwhile, heat the sesame oil in a wok, then add the chilli and the remaining vegetables and stir-fry. When cooked, stir in the reserved marinade, cook for 30 seconds and then stir through the noodles and half of the sesame seeds.

5. Remove the duck breasts from the oven and cut into slices on the diagonal.

6. To serve, arrange the vegetables and noodles on 4 plates, place the sliced duck breast on top and garnish with the remaining sesame seeds and the fresh coriander leaves.

LINGUINE WITH PEAS

Children love this fresh, simple recipe that can be adapted according to what is available (the addition of chopped crisp bacon is particularly good). The use of crème fraîche makes for a delicious creamy sauce that tastes rather like spaghetti carbonara. Crème fraîche is high in fat, so it will not curdle when heated. Serve with a tomato salad and crusty bread.

Preparation and cooking time: 15 minutes
Serves 4

450g/1lb dried linguine pasta   *salt and fresh ground black pepper*
225g/8oz frozen peas
150ml/¼ pint crème fraîche   *To garnish*
2 tablespoons roughly chopped   *Parmesan cheese shavings*
* fresh basil*   *basil leaves*

1. Cook the linguine in plenty of rapidly boiling salted water.

2. Meanwhile, cook the peas in a little salted boiling water. Drain.

3. When the linguine is just cooked, drain it, then return it to the saucepan

with the peas, crème fraîche, chopped basil and salt and pepper. Mix together well.

4. Pile on to a serving dish, garnish with the Parmesan and basil leaves, and serve immediately.

SMOKED SALMON PASTA

This is a simple pasta dish that takes no time at all to make. Crème fraîche is a truly useful ingredient: it heats well without splitting so can be used in many recipes that call for a creamy white sauce.

Preparation time: 5–10 minutes
Cooking time: 10 minutes
Serves 4

400g/14oz pasta
225g/8oz mangetout, cut diagonally in half
1 tub half-fat crème fraîche
juice of ½ a lemon
salt and freshly ground pepper

225g/8oz smoked salmon, cut into strips

To garnish
chopped chives

1. Cook the pasta in plenty of boiling water according to the manufacturer's instructions. Add the mangetout 2 minutes before the end of the cooking time.

2. Meanwhile, heat the crème fraîche in a small saucepan. Add the lemon juice and plenty of salt and pepper.

3. Drain the pasta and mangetout. Pour the warm crème fraîche over the pasta and add the smoked salmon. Stir gently and serve immediately, garnished with the chopped chives.

PASTA WITH TOMATOES AND BACON

This recipe could not be easier to make. If you cannot get sunblushed tomatoes use sundried. If you cannot buy sunblushed tomatoes in oil, use flavoured oil instead – lemon oil gives a wonderfully clean, fresh taste.

Preparation time: 10 minutes
Cooking time: 12 minutes
Serves 4

400g/14oz pasta (for example, *tagliatelle*)
1 × 170g/6oz pack of lardons
110g/4oz sunblushed tomatoes, in oil, sliced

55g/2oz Parmesan cheese, freshly grated
handful of fresh basil leaves, torn
salt and freshly ground black pepper

1. Cook the pasta in a large pan of boiling salted water until tender.
2. Meanwhile, fry the lardons in a heavy saucepan until golden brown.
3. Drain the pasta and return to the pan off the heat. Add the lardons, tomatoes, Parmesan, basil and some of the tomato oil to the pasta. Season with salt and pepper.
4. Serve immediately garnished with extra basil.

MUSHROOM AND MUSTARD PASTA

This is a very quick supper dish – the sauce is rich and creamy but far easier to make than a classic white sauce.

Preparation time: 5 minutes
Cooking time: 20 minutes
Serves 4–6

450g/1lb mixed mushrooms, such as chestnut, closed cup, portobello, sliced
2 tablespoons oil
200ml/7fl oz crème fraîche
2 teaspoons Dijon mustard
2 teaspoons grainy mustard

salt and freshly ground black pepper
450g/1lb dried penne
2 tablespoons tarragon, freshly chopped

To garnish
Parmesan cheese shavings

1. Heat the oil in a frying pan and fry the mushrooms in batches until just cooked. Remove from the pan and set aside.
2. Add the crème fraîche to the frying pan and slowly bring to the boil. Mix in the mustards.

3. Return the mushrooms to the sauce and reheat. Season to taste.
4. Meanwhile, cook the pasta in plenty of rapidly boiling salted water. Drain well and mix with the sauce.
5. Add the tarragon. Pile the pasta on to a serving dish and sprinkle with Parmesan cheese.

ARTICHOKE, FETA AND CHERVIL TAGLIATELLE

This pasta dish is very quick and easy to prepare. If chervil is not available, use very finely chopped fresh parsley instead. It must be made at the last minute, as the sauce does not keep warm well.

Preparation time: 15 minutes
Cooking time: 10 minutes
Serves 2–3

225g/8oz dried tagliatelle
1 × 285g/10oz jar artichoke
  hearts, drained and halved
finely grated zest of 2 lemons
170g/6oz feta cheese, cut into
  1.25cm/½in cubes
55g/2oz chervil, roughly chopped

290ml/½ pint soured cream
salt and freshly ground black
  pepper

To serve
85g/3oz Parmesan cheese, freshly
  grated

1. Bring a large pan of salted water to the boil and cook the tagliatelle according to the manufacturer's instructions.
2. Meanwhile, mix together the artichokes, lemon zest, feta and chervil. Set aside.

3. Drain the pasta and return to the hot pan, stir in the soured cream and season well with salt and black pepper.
4. Add the artichoke and feta mixture to the pan and mix well.
5. Serve the pasta in warmed bowls, sprinkled with the Parmesan cheese.

SPAGHETTI WITH LEMON, ROCKET AND PARMESAN

This is a very quick pasta dish that can be prepared at the last minute. The recipe calls for lemon oil but if it is unavailable use a little extra lemon zest. Serve with a green salad and plenty of crusty white bread.

Preparation time: 5 minutes
Cooking time: 15 minutes
Serves 4

400g/14oz spaghetti
2 tablespoons lemon oil
2 cloves garlic, crushed
zest of 1 lemon
110g/4oz rocket, washed

salt and freshly ground black pepper

To serve
55g/2oz Parmesan cheese
shavings

1. Bring a large pan of salted water to the boil and cook the spaghetti according to the manufacturer's instructions.
2. Heat the oil in a small, heavy-based pan. Sauté the garlic gently to release the flavour but be careful not to brown it.
3. Drain the spaghetti. Add the oil, garlic, lemon zest and rocket. Season with salt and pepper. Pile it on to a serving dish and sprinkle with the Parmesan shavings.

PEA, ASPARAGUS AND FRENCH BEAN PASTA

This is one of the easiest pasta dishes that I know and there is not even any washing up at the end of the cooking process! Frozen peas can easily be used instead of fresh ones. A few blanched asparagus tips can be reserved and used as a garnish if required.

Preparation time: 10 minutes
Cooking time: 10 minutes
Serves 4

400g/14oz pasta
110g/4oz garden peas, blanched
  and refreshed
110g/4oz French beans, blanched
  and refreshed
55g/2oz asparagus tips, blanched
  and refreshed
3 tablespoons olive oil

2 tablespoons crème fraîche
  (optional)
½ tablespoon mint, freshly
  chopped
salt and freshly ground black
  pepper

To garnish
Parmesan cheese shavings

1. Cook the pasta in a large pan of boiling salted water according to the manufacturer's instructions. Add the vegetables to the water 30 seconds before the end of the cooking time.
2. Drain the pasta and vegetables.
3. Stir through the olive oil, crème fraîche, if using, and mint and season well with salt and freshly ground black pepper. Garnish with the Parmesan and serve immediately.

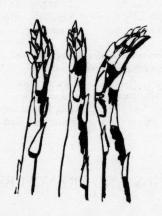

HOT BUTTERED SHALLOTS WITH GOAT'S CHEESE

This dish can be served as a first course or as an accompaniment to a main course. It is popular with children because the onions become sweet as they bake. Try to buy shallots rather than button onions: they have a milder, less bitter flavour which marries well with the sage and goat's cheese. To peel the shallots, put them into a bowl and cover with boiling water. Leave to stand for 2–3 minutes and remove with a slotted spoon. If the skin does not come off easily, return to the bowl of hot water for a further 1–2 minutes.

The shallots can be baked a day in advance and then grilled at the last minute.

Preparation time: 20 minutes
Cooking time: 40 minutes
Serves 4

*675g/1½lb shallots or button
  onions, peeled
110g/4oz unsalted butter, diced
3 tablespoons dry white wine*

*salt and freshly ground black pepper
1 tablespoon caster sugar
2 tablespoons fresh chopped sage
200g/7oz goat's cheese, crumbled*

1. Preheat the oven to 180°C/350°F/gas mark 4. Preheat the grill.
2. Put the shallots and butter into a shallow ovenproof dish. Cover with the wine, and season with the salt and pepper. Add the caster sugar and half of the sage.
3. Place in the oven and bake for 30 minutes or until the shallots are tender and caramelised. Remove from the oven.
4. Crumble the goat's cheese, then place it on top of the shallots with the remaining sage. Place under the grill until brown and bubbling, then serve.

MOROCCAN-STYLE FILO PIE

When we recipe tested this recipe it was universally popular. It is simple to make and can be completely assembled in advance and then frozen or baked as required.

Preparation time: 20 minutes
Cooking time: 15 minutes
Serves 4

2 tablespoons olive oil
1 red onion, sliced
1 × 400g/14oz can chopped
* tomatoes with chilli*
150ml/¼ pint water or stock
1 × 400g/14oz can mixed
* cooked pulses, drained and*
* rinsed*

110g/4oz dried dates, chopped
1 tablespoon chopped fresh flat-
* leaf parsley*
salt and freshly ground black
* pepper*
5 sheets filo pastry
55g/2oz butter, melted with a
* large pinch of cinnamon*

1. Preheat the oven to 200°C/400°F/gas mark 6.
2. Heat the oil in a heavy-based saucepan, add the onion and cook slowly until soft. Add the tomatoes, stock and pulses. Season with salt and pepper, bring to the boil and simmer for 6–7 minutes, stirring occasionally. Add the dates and parsley, mix well and turn into a casserole dish.
3. Cover the pie with 5 layers of filo pastry, brushing each layer with the melted butter and cinnamon.
4. Bake for 15 minutes or until the pastry is golden brown.

BAKED MUSHROOMS WITH SUNDRIED TOMATOES AND CHEESE

These mushrooms are simple to make and are ideal as a snack or first course. They can be prepared to the end of step 3 well in advance and then baked just before you are ready to serve.

Preparation time: 5 minutes
Cooking time: 20–25 minutes
Serves 4 as a first course

4 very large field mushrooms
olive oil
8 sundried tomatoes, cut in half
2 big sprigs fresh basil, roughly
* chopped*

salt and freshly ground black
* pepper*
30g/1oz Cheddar cheese, freshly
* grated*

1. Preheat the oven to 200°C/400°F/gas mark 6.
2. Trim the stalks from the mushrooms. Place the mushrooms on a baking sheet, gills-side up. Drizzle the gills with a little olive oil, season with salt and pepper and bake for 10 minutes. Finely chop the mushroom stalks.
3. Remove the mushrooms from the oven. Top each mushroom with 4 pieces of tomato, the finely chopped mushroom stalks, the basil and lastly the grated cheese.
4. Return to the oven for a further 10 minutes or until the mushrooms are cooked and the cheese is lightly browned.

BUTTERNUT SQUASH, RED ONION AND THYME RISOTTO

A risotto normally takes about 40 minutes of carefully monitored cooking. It is essential that the stock is hot, otherwise it will take even longer to cook – the restaurateurs' trick is to add ¾ of the stock and then to take the risotto off the heat. When you are ready to serve, reheat the risotto and gradually add the remaining hot stock. You may need more stock than the recipe calls for.

Preparation time: 15 minutes
Cooking time: 40 minutes
Serves 4

2 tablespoons olive oil
2 medium red onions, chopped
225g/8oz butternut squash, peeled and finely diced
2 cloves garlic, crushed
340g/12oz arborio risotto rice
1 glass white wine
pinch of saffron

820–860ml/1¼–1½ pints hot vegetable stock or hot water
2 tablespoons fresh thyme, chopped
30g/1oz butter
salt and pepper
Parmesan cheese, grated, to taste

1. Heat the oil in a sauté pan, add the red onions and sweat for 15 minutes. Add the squash and cook for a further 10 minutes. Add the garlic and rice, and stir until the rice looks a little translucent.
2. Add the glass of wine – it may sizzle – and, when absorbed, add the saffron.

3. Stir in approximately ¼ of the hot stock or water, stirring occasionally until absorbed, then continue to add more stock or water, stirring occasionally, until the risotto has a creamy texture but the rice still retains a 'bite' – this will take about 25 minutes.
4. Stir in the thyme, butter, salt and pepper and grated Parmesan to taste.
5. Serve sprinkled with a little extra Parmesan.

SUMMER VEGETABLE RISOTTO

Make the most of summer's bounty with this delicious fresh vegetable risotto. Any combination of vegetables can be used; choose the freshest available. Grate your Parmesan from a wedge of Reggiano Parmesan for the best flavour.

To cook the onions quickly, chop them finely and place in a microwave bowl with a tablespoon of oil. Cover with clingfilm and microwave on high for three minutes. Let stand for 2 minutes, then use as required. This recipe can be prepared in advance to the end of step 6; the remaining stock and vegetables should be added when you are ready to eat. Serve with hot crusty bread and a green salad.

Preparation time: 10 minutes
Cooking time: 30 minutes
Serves 4 as a main course or 8 as a first course

30g/1oz butter
1 large onion, chopped
1.2 litres/2 pints hot vegetable stock
large pinch saffron strands
  (optional)
110g/4oz each of any 4 of the
  following: fresh peas,
  asparagus, carrots, broad
  beans, French beans, runner
  beans, courgettes

340g/12oz risotto rice
110ml/4fl oz white wine
salt and freshly ground black
  pepper
6 tablespoons freshly grated
  Parmesan plus extra for
  shavings

To garnish
1 tablespoon chopped fresh
  parsley

1. Melt the butter in a large sauté pan. Stir in the onion and cook over low heat until soft (or cook in the microwave as described above).
2. Place the stock in a saucepan and bring to the simmer. Add the saffron strands and keep hot.
3. Cut the vegetables into 2.5cm/1in cubes or pieces.
4. Tip the rice into the pan with the onion and stir for 1 minute to coat with the butter.
5. Pour in the wine and stir until it has evaporated.
6. Stir a ladleful of the hot stock into the rice. When the stock has nearly evaporated, add another ladleful.
7. When half of the stock has been added, tip in all the vegetables except the courgettes if using. Continue adding the stock by stirring in a ladleful at a time.
8. When nearly all the stock has been added, stir in the courgettes. The risotto is done when the rice is cooked through but still has some 'bite'.
9. Stir in the grated Parmesan and season as required. Serve immediately, garnished with the parsley and Parmesan shavings.

PEA, BACON AND CAMBOZOLA RISOTTO

A risotto should be made at the last minute, because it will not sit well. Make sure that the stock is hot when you add it, in order to maintain the temperature of the risotto. The quantity of stock is a little by and large – if necessary a little hot water can be added at the end.

Preparation time: 30 minutes
Cooking time: 25–30 minutes
Serves 4

2 tablespoons olive oil
1 medium onion, chopped
1 garlic clove, crushed
200g/7oz bacon, chopped
200g/7oz button mushrooms,
  finely sliced
340g/12oz arborio risotto rice

1 glass white wine
825–860ml/1¼–1½ pints hot
  chicken stock
250g/8oz frozen garden peas or
  petit pois
170g/6oz Cambozola cheese,
  cubed
salt and pepper

1. Heat the oil in a large pan, add the onions and sweat for 15 minutes.
Add the bacon and fry until the fat has rendered down and the bacon is
cooked. Add the mushrooms and cook until any liquid has been driven off,
then add the garlic and cook for 30 seconds. Add the rice and stir.
2. Add the glass of wine – at this point the contents of the pan may sizzle.
3. Add the hot stock, a little at a time, stirring until the liquid is absorbed.
Take care not to stir more than necessary – you don't want to make the
risotto mushy. However, stir enough to incorporate the stock and to
prevent the risotto from catching on the bottom of the pan. Continue to stir
in more stock until the risotto is a creamy texture but the rice still retains its
'bite' – this will take about 25–30 minutes.
4. Add the peas, stir and leave for 1 minute. Stir in the Cambozola, and salt
and pepper to taste. Leave to rest for 3 minutes, to allow the cheese to melt.
Serve immediately.

CHEESE FONDUE

Cheese fondue is perfect for a cold winter's evening. It doesn't require
the use of a special fondue set – simply use a good-quality heavy
saucepan. It should be kept warm while your guests are serving
themselves. Serve with cubes of French bread, or raw vegetables as
'dippers', a green salad and plenty of white wine.

Preparation time: 10 minutes
Cooking time: 20 minutes
Serves 4

1 clove garlic, peeled and cut in
  half
juice of ½ lemon
240ml/8fl oz dry white wine
125g/4½oz Gruyère cheese,
  grated

125g/4½oz Emmental cheese,
  grated
2 tablespoons kirsch
2 teaspoons cornflour
salt and pepper
grated nutmeg

1. Rub the garlic clove over the base and sides of a heavy saucepan.
2. Put the lemon juice and white wine into the pan and gradually bring to
the boil.
3. Add the cheese to the pan and allow it to melt gently, then bring the
mixture up to the boil. If it begins to go lumpy, increase the heat slightly.
4. Mix the kirsch and cornflour together and add to the fondue mix – it
should thicken and become smooth.
5. Add the salt, pepper and nutmeg and keep warm.

GNOCCHI WITH GOAT'S CHEESE AND SUNDRIED TOMATOES

This is a simple salad – the gnocchi can be cooked a day in advance
and kept refrigerated in oil. Frying the gnocchi means that it is not as
stodgy as it would be if it was simply cooked and then mixed with the
salad ingredients.

Preparation time: 5 minutes
Cooking time: 10 minutes
Serves 4

1 × 400g/14oz packet gnocchi
1 tablespoon olive oil
110g/4oz sundried tomatoes,
  sliced, with their oil reserved

110g/4oz goat's cheese, roughly
  chopped
55g/2oz pitted black olives
30g/1oz pinenuts, toasted
½ bunch basil, roughly chopped

1. Cook the gnocchi according to the manufacturer's instructions. Drain
well and dry.
2. Heat the oil in a heavy frying pan, add the gnocchi and fry until golden
brown.

3. Reduce the heat, add the sundried tomatoes, goat's cheese and olives and mix through thoroughly until the cheese has practically melted.
4. Finally, mix in the pinenuts and basil.
5. Serve immediately with a drizzling of the reserved tomato oil.

MARINATED HALLOUMI

Halloumi is a Middle Eastern curd cheese that holds its shape when heated. It has a distinct texture, that can only be described as squeaky. It is available in all good supermarkets. This griddled halloumi is delicious served as a first course – alternatively, arranged on one large plate, without the salad it can be served as a part of a collection of tapas alternatives such as salted almonds, marinated anchovies and black olives.

Preparation time: 5 minutes (plus marinating time)
Cooking time 10 minutes
Serves 4

Pared zest and juice of 1 lemon
5 tablespoons olive oil
5 basil leaves, torn
freshly ground black pepper
1 × 250g/8½oz pack halloumi
  cheese, cut into 1cm/½in slices

To serve
1 large ripe tomato, peeled and
  chopped
green salad

1. Mix together the lemon zest and juice with the olive oil, basil and black pepper. Place the halloumi in a shallow dish and pour the dressing over the top. Leave to marinate for as long as possible.
2. When ready to serve, remove the halloumi from the dressing. Taste the dressing and adjust any seasoning, then stir in the chopped tomatoes.
3. Heat a heavy-based frying pan and fry the halloumi on both sides until golden brown.
4. Arrange the green salad on 4 plates. Place the halloumi slices over the salad and drizzle the dressing over the top.

VEGETABLE DISHES

OVEN-DRIED PLUM TOMATOES

This is a homemade version of sunblush tomatoes. If you want to dry them, leave to cool completely for about another 6 hours. The timing and temperature are approximate – they depend on the size of the tomatoes and the accuracy of your oven – so check the progress every 2–3 hours. If you have an Aga, the slow oven is the ideal place in which to dry the tomatoes.

Preparation time: 10 minutes
Cooking time: 18 hours

1.8kg/4lb plum tomatoes
5 cloves garlic, sliced
1 tablespoon chopped fresh
  thyme

salt and freshly ground black
  pepper
olive oil
balsamic vinegar

1. Preheat the oven to 130°C/250°F/gas mark 1.
2. Cut the tomatoes in half lengthways.
3. Place the tomatoes cut-side up in a single layer on a wire rack over a roasting tray.
4. Sprinkle the garlic, thyme, salt and pepper over the tomatoes and drizzle with a little olive oil and balsamic vinegar.
5. Place in the oven and leave for 18 hours.

LEMON AND THYME BAKED POTATOES

The deliciousness of this dish – and it is delicious – is dependent on using very good new potatoes such as Charlottes. The caramelised lemon acts as a great accompaniment to fish, or cuts through the fat of roast duck.

675g/1½lb small new potatoes
2 lemons, quartered lengthways
4 sprigs fresh thyme

coarse sea salt and freshly ground
  black pepper
2 tablespoons olive oil

1. Preheat the oven to 200°C/400°F/gas mark 6.
2. Put the potatoes into a large, shallow roasting tin. Squeeze the lemon quarters gently to release a little of their juice over the potatoes and then add them to the tin.
3. Lay the sprigs of thyme on top of the potatoes and season with sea salt and black pepper. Cover with the olive oil.
4. Bake the potatoes, stirring occasionally, in the centre of the preheated oven for 1–1½ hours or until the potatoes are tender and the lemons caramelised.
5. Remove the sprigs of thyme from the pan and serve.

CRACKED WHEAT AND CHICKPEA SALAD

This must be one of the easiest recipes that we cook at Leith's – it is our standby instant lunch for unexpected guests. It requires only basic ingredients that we always have in the store room and takes very little skill to make. To add moisture to the finished salad, add as much oil from the sundried tomato jar as you can. Serve it with some nice salamis, a green salad and hot French bread for a spring lunch.

Preparation time: 10 minutes.
Serves 4

170g/6oz fine cracked wheat
1 × 400g/14oz can chickpeas
1 × 190g/6½oz jar red pesto
½ bunch coriander, washed and
  roughly chopped

4 sundried tomatoes, very finely
  chopped
salt and freshly ground black
  pepper

1. Prepare the cracked wheat according to the manufacturer's instructions.
2. Allow the cracked wheat to dry.
3. Rinse the chickpeas and pat dry.
4. Mix together the cracked wheat and chickpeas with the red pesto, chopped coriander and sundried tomatoes. Season to taste with salt and freshly ground black pepper.

SOUFFLÉD JACKET POTATOES

This simple recipe is perfect when the cupboard and fridge seem empty. The soufflé part makes a change from the run-of-mill jacket potato, and makes an easy supper dish appear quite glamorous. For variations on the basic recipe, use different cheeses or add ham.

Preparation time: 10 minutes
Cooking time: 1¼ hours
Serves 4

4 baking potatoes, scrubbed
oil
sea salt and freshly ground black
  pepper
2 eggs, separated
2 tablespoons double cream

200g/7oz ball buffalo mozzarella
  cheese, diced
85g/3oz Parmesan cheese, freshly
  grated
small bunch of chives, snipped

1. Preheat the oven to 200°C/400°F/gas mark 6.
2. Rub the potatoes with the oil and sprinkle with a little salt. Bake for 1 hour or until very tender.
3. Cut the potatoes in half lengthways. Scoop pit the soft centres and place in a large mixing bowl. Set the skins aside.
4. Season the potato with salt and pepper, add the egg yolks and cream and beat together thoroughly. Stir in the diced mozzarella, half of the Parmesan and the chives.
5. In a separate bowl, work the egg whites until medium peaks are formed. Fold them into the potato mixture and pile it back into the potato skins.
6. Sprinkle with the remaining Parmesan and return the potatoes to the oven for 15 minutes or until hot, risen and golden brown. Serve immediately.

KHAPOLI POTATOES

These delicious Middle Eastern potatoes make a perfect accompaniment to meat dishes but can also be served as a simple first course.

Preparation time: 15 minutes
Cooking time: 5 minutes
Serves 6

2 tablespoons sunflower oil	1 green chilli, finely chopped
1 teaspoon cumin seeds	sugar
8–10 curry leaves	salt
900g/2lb potatoes, cubed and parboiled	grated zest and juice of 1 lime
2.5cm/1in piece fresh root ginger, peeled and chopped to a purée	To garnish
	chopped fresh coriander

1. Heat the oil in a frying pan and add the cumin seeds and curry leaves. Add the potatoes and cook gently.
2. Add the ginger and chilli. Increase the heat and fry for 2–3 minutes. Add sugar and salt to taste and the lime zest and juice.
3. Add the coriander and serve immediately.

PUSHPA'S SOUTH INDIAN DAHL

This delicious dahl is simple to make and should be served warm with pitta bread or as an accompaniment to curries. To make the garlic and ginger purées, simply peel the garlic or ginger and chop to a pulp; alternatively, 'cheat' purées can be bought in most supermarkets.

Preparation time: 15 minutes
Cooking time: 30 minutes
Serves 4–6

225g/8oz orange lentils	handful of fresh coriander leaves, chopped
1–2 onions, sliced	
2 teaspoons garlic purée	1–2 extra onions, thinly sliced, for frying
2 teaspoons ginger purée	
oil	6 cloves garlic, sliced
2 teaspoons ground coriander	1–2 teaspoons whole cumin seeds
2 teaspoons ground cumin	1–2 teaspoons mustard seeds
1 teaspoon ground turmeric	about 10 curry leaves
6 tomatoes, peeled and chopped	salt
1 level teaspoon ground chilli	

1. Wash the lentils, then put them into a large saucepan with half the onions. Add water to cover, then add the garlic and ginger purées and 1 tablespoon of oil.
2. Place over the heat and when the mixture begins to boil add the ground spices, tomatoes, chilli, salt and half of the coriander. Simmer for 15–20 minutes.
3. While this is simmering, heat 2 tablespoons of oil in a frying pan. Add the remaining onions and fry until pale brown, then add the garlic and fry for 5 minutes. Finally, add the cumin seeds, mustard seeds and curry leaves.
4. When the mixture is dark brown in colour, add it to the dahl mixture.
5. Serve garnished with the remaining coriander.

PESTO-BAKED SWEET POTATOES

This must be one of our easiest and yet most delicious recipes. These potatoes are delicious eaten with barbecued food and are perfect on a Sunday evening with cold meats and chutneys.

Preparation time: 10 minutes
Cooking time: 1¼ hours
Serves 4

4 large sweet potatoes
3 tablespoons pesto
4 tablespoons Parmesan cheese,
   freshly grated

salt and freshly ground black
   pepper

1. Preheat the oven to 200°C/400°F/gas mark 6.
2. Wash the potatoes and cut them in half lengthwise with a sharp knife, then make a deep lattice pattern on the flesh side of the potatoes.

3. Season the potatoes with salt and black pepper and bake in the centre of the preheated oven for 50–60 minutes.

4. Remove the potatoes from the oven and cover with the pesto sauce. Sprinkle with the Parmesan and return to the oven for a further 10–15 minutes or until very tender. Serve hot.

JERSEY ROYAL SALAD

This salad is particularly good if the potatoes are still warm when mixed with the dressing. There is always a problem making a salad with red beetroot as it colours all the other vegetables – if golden beetroot is available do use it – the essential thing is to cook the beetroot yourself – steam or boil in its skin for 1–1½ hours, allow to cool and then peel.

Preparation time: 35 minutes
Serves 4

1 tablespoon oil
12oz/340g Jersey Royals cooked,
  halved if necessary
150g/5oz broad beans, cooked
  and shelled
150g/5oz peas, cooked
1 beetroot, cooked, peeled and
  diced
4 slices Parma ham, grilled until
  crisp

4 poached eggs
salt and freshly ground black
  pepper

For the dressing
3 tablespoons crème fraîche
4 teaspoons balsamic vinegar
1 tablespoon fresh mint, finely
  chopped
salt and freshly ground black
  pepper

1. Mix together the ingredients for the dressing and season with salt and pepper.

2. Mix together the potatoes, broad beans and peas and add the dressing. Season well with salt and freshly ground pepper. Divide between 4 plates.

3. Quickly mix through the beetroot to get a marbled effect.

4. Divide the salad between 4 plates. Top each portion with a poached egg and cover with the Parma ham.

LEMON AND SOURED CREAM MASH

Preparation time: 10 minutes
Cooking time: 25 minutes
Serves 4

*675g/1½lb potatoes, peeled and
cut into chunks
grated zest of 2 lemons*

*150ml/¼ pint soured cream
salt and freshly ground black
pepper*

1. Boil the potatoes in salted water for 10–15 minutes or until tender. Drain thoroughly. Push the potatoes through a sieve or mouli and return them to the dry saucepan.
2. Heat carefully, stirring to allow the potatoes to steam dry.
3. Beat in the lemon zest and soured cream. Season to taste with salt and pepper. Serve hot.

GEM SQUASH WITH MUSHROOMS

These stuffed gem squash can be served as a generous first course or as a supper dish. If serving as a supper dish, we would recommend them with hot garlic bread and a crisp green salad. They make a particularly good vegetarian meal.

Preparation time: 30 minutes
Cooking time; 20 minutes
Serves 4

4 gem squash
1 tablespoon oil
2 red onions, finely chopped
2 cloves garlic, crushed
450g/1lb mushrooms, sliced
2 tablespoons lemon thyme,
  chopped

4 tablespoons crème fraîche
salt and freshly ground black
  pepper

To serve
Parmesan cheese shavings

1. Heat the oil in a large saucepan, add the onions and sweat until soft.
Add the garlic and cook for 45 seconds, then add the mushrooms and allow
to cook until softened and any water has evaporated.
2. Meanwhile, cut the tops off the gem squash and scoop out the seeds and
stringy centres. Bring a large pan of salted water to the boil and boil the
squash and their tops for 10–15 minutes or until just tender.
3. Add the lemon thyme and crème fraîche to the mushroom mixture and
stir through. Season with salt and pepper and allow to reduce, by boiling
rapidly, until the sauce is creamy.
4. Season the inside of the squash lightly and generously pile the mushroom
filling into them. Sprinkle with the Parmesan cheese, replace the squash
tops and serve immediately.

PANCETTA AND CAULIFLOWER CHEESE

This is cauliflower cheese with a difference. Pancetta is a particularly
delicious bacon readily available in most supermarkets. The addition of
bacon means that the cauliflower can be served as a supper dish
simply with a green salad and some chunky white bread.

Many supermarkets sell individual cauliflowers – if using, allow one
tiny cauliflower per head. This dish can be made a day in advance and
then reheated and grilled, but it does not freeze well.

Preparation time: 10 minutes
Cooking time: 15 minutes
Serves 4

1 large or 2 small cauliflowers
110g/4oz pancetta, cut into
   chunks
20g/¾oz butter
20g/¾oz plain flour
pinch dry English mustard
   powder

pinch cayenne pepper
290ml/½ pint milk
55g/2oz Gruyère or strong
   Cheddar cheese, grated
1 teaspoon dried white
   breadcrumbs
1 tablespoon Cheddar cheese,
   grated

1. Break the cauliflower into florets and cook in boiling salted water until just tender. Drain well.

2. Fry the pancetta over a medium flame until golden brown. Remove from the pan with a slotted spoon and drain on kitchen paper.

3. Preheat the grill.

4. Melt the butter in a heavy saucepan and stir in the flour, mustard and cayenne pepper. Cook, stirring, for 1 minute, then remove the pan from the heat. Pour in the milk and mix well.

5. Return the pan to the heat and stir until boiling. Simmer, stirring well, for 2 minutes. Add 55g/2oz of cheese and mix well, but do not allow the sauce to re-boil. Season to taste with salt and pepper. Stir in the pancetta.

6. Put the cauliflower into an ovenproof dish and coat with the sauce. Sprinkle with the breadcrumbs and the remaining tablespoon of Cheddar cheese and place under the hot grill until brown.

PARSNIP AND POTATO DAUPHINOISE

This delicious creamy dauphinoise has a naturally sweet flavour and is therefore an ideal accompaniment for a rich meat such as lamb, beef or venison. It can be prepared a day in advance and baked when required.

Preparation time: 25 minutes
Cooking time: 1½ hours
Serves 4–6

1 tablespoon oil
1 medium onion, sliced
1 clove garlic, crushed
1 teaspoon plain flour
340g/12oz parsnips, peeled and
   thinly sliced

570g/1¼lb old potatoes, peeled
   and thinly sliced
570ml/1 pint double cream
salt and freshly ground black
   pepper

1. Preheat the oven to 170°C/325°F/gas mark 3.
2. Heat the oil in a large saucepan. Add the onion and cook until soft but not coloured, add the garlic and cook for a further 45 seconds (do not burn). Add the flour and cook for 1 minute.
3. Add the parsnips, potatoes and cream, and season with salt and pepper. Bring to the boil, then simmer for 5 minutes.
4. Pour the potato, parsnip and cream mix into a large ovenproof dish.
5. Cook in the preheated oven for 1–1½ hours or until tender.

DRUNKEN BEANS

In this delicious Latin American recipe the beans are left whole and cooked in a mixture of spices and beer until there is almost no liquid left. These drunken beans can replace refried beans as a filling for tacos, burritos, tostadas and the like.

Preparation time: 10 minues
Cooking time: 1 hour 15 minutes
Serves 6

1 tablespoon sunflower oil
3 rashers rindless streaky smoked
    bacon, chopped
1 large onion, finely chopped
2 cloves garlic, crushed
1 teaspoon ground cumin
1 teaspoon chilli powder or 1
    teaspoon crushed chillies
1 teaspoon freshly chopped
    oregano

2 × 400g/14oz cans cooked
    pinto beans
1 × 400g/14oz can chopped
    tomatoes
190ml/⅓ pint light beer
190ml/⅓ pint water
salt and freshly ground black
    pepper

1. In a large saucepan, heat the oil and cook the bacon for 3 minutes. Add the onion, garlic, cumin, chilli and oregano and cook, stirring from time to time, until the onion is nearly soft, about 10 minutes.
2. Add the cooked beans, tomatoes, beer and water and mix thoroughly. Season with salt and pepper and bring to the boil. Reduce the heat and simmer, covered, for 30 minutes.
3. Remove the lid, stir well and simmer for a further 20 minutes or until there is very little liquid left. Season to taste with salt and pepper and serve hot.

BEAN AND PARSLEY MASH

This delicious mash is wonderful served with grilled chicken or steak – but it needs to be well seasoned. Do not mash the beans too much, because the final mixture should retain some texture. If cannellini beans are unavailable, then any other white bean can be used – butter beans are particularly good. The herb can be varied according to taste and what you are going to serve the mash with. If it's fish, then use dill, tarragon, chervil instead of parsley; if it's chicken, then finely chopped thyme or rosemary can be used.

Preparation time: 10 minutes
Cooking time: 25 minutes
Serves 4

150ml/¼ pint good quality olive oil
1 onion, chopped
4 cloves garlic, crushed
2 × 400g/14oz cans cannellini beans, drained and rinsed

20g/¾oz parsley, finely chopped
juice and zest of 1 lemon
salt and freshly ground black pepper

1. Heat the olive oil in a pan, add the onion and cook on a low heat until soft. Add the garlic and cook for a further 2 minutes.
2. Stir through the beans, lemon juice and zest and mash with the back of a fork.
3. Add the parsley and season to taste.

CORN ON THE COB WITH CHILLI BUTTER

Corn on the cob seems to be universally popular – and this version, served with a chilli- and coriander-flavoured butter, transforms it from the humdrum to the exotic. The butter can be made in advance and then frozen and defrosted when required. The butter can also be used with baby sweetcorn, grilled chicken, fish and steaks, and is particularly good with baked potatoes.

Be careful not to overcook sweetcorn: it toughens if cooked for longer than 10 minutes. It will also be tougher if cooked in salted water.

151

Preparation time: 10 minutes
Cooking time: 8–10 minutes
Serves 4

4 corn on the cob

For the butter
55g/2oz butter, softened
½–1 red chilli, finely chopped
zest of 1 lime, grated

juice of ½ a lime
2 tablespoons fresh, finely
*   chopped coriander*
salt and freshly ground black
*   pepper*
1.25cm/½in fresh ginger, peeled
*   and grated (optional)*

1. Prepare the flavoured butter: put the butter into a small bowl, add the remaining ingredients and mix together well.
2. Wrap the mixture into greaseproof paper or clingfilm and roll into a fat cylinder. Refrigerate.
3. Bring a large pan of water to the boil, add the corn and cook until tender, about 5–10 minutes. Drain.
4. Cut the butter into slices and serve it separately to the corn so that guests may use as much or as little as they require. As the butter melts it will flavour the corn.

PUDDINGS

FRENCH TOAST WITH BRAMBLES

This is a variation on the popular theme of eggy bread – it can either be served as a pudding with the brambles or eaten plain or with some crisp bacon for breakfast. Any red or black, fresh or frozen soft fruits can be used in place of brambles; if using frozen fruits, defrost them on a flat tray sprinkled with a little caster sugar for 2–3 hours.

Preparation time: 10 minutes
Cooking time: 20 minutes
Serves 4

4 slices of day-old white bread,
   2.5cm/1in thick, crusts removed
55g/2oz unsalted butter
caster sugar for sprinkling

For the custard
1 large egg
1 egg yolk
55g/2oz soft light brown sugar
150ml/¼ pint full-cream milk
1 tablespoon Calvados

For the glaze
45g/1½oz unsalted butter
85g/3oz soft light brown sugar
4 tablespoons cider
3 tablespoons apple juice
1 tablespoon Calvados
2 tablespoons double cream
450g/1lb brambles, washed

To serve
icing sugar

1. Make the custard: put the egg and egg yolk into a large shallow dish, add the sugar and mix well. Add the milk and Calvados.
2. Put the slices of bread into the custard for 5 minutes, turning them over once.

153

3. Melt the butter in a large frying pan. When it is foaming, fry the slices of bread until golden brown on both sides. Drain on absorbent kitchen paper and sprinkle with a little caster sugar. Keep warm.

4. Meanwhile, make the glaze: melt the unsalted butter in a small saucepan. Add the sugar, cider, apple juice and Calvados. Bring to the boil and simmer for 1–2 minutes or until syrupy and reduced by half its original quantity. Stir in the double cream.

5. Add the brambles to the saucepan and mix to coat them thoroughly with the glaze. Keep warm.

6. Put the warm fried bread on to individual serving plates. Pile on the brambles and pour the glaze over the top. Dust with icing sugar and serve immediately.

KIR ROYALE JELLIES WITH BLACKBERRIES

This pudding is for a special occasion, but it's suprisingly easy to get a spectacular result. Kir Royale is a combination of crème de cassis and champagne, but still wine as a champagne substitute can be used in this recipe. Do not be afraid of using leaf gelatine: it is now readily available in most supermarkets, it gives a clearer jelly and is far easier to use than the powdered type. The alcohol is not completely boiled away in this recipe, so be careful when calculating your units before driving home.

Preparation and chilling time: 4 hours
Serves 4

6 leaves of gelatine
150ml/¼ pint cold water
570ml/1 pint sparkling white wine
5 tablespoons crème de cassis
110g/4oz caster sugar

110g/4oz blackberries, washed and picked over

To garnish
mint sprigs

1. Soak the gelatine in the cold water for 5 minutes or until softened.

2. Meanwhile, put the wine, crème de cassis and sugar into a saucepan and heat gently until the sugar has dissolved. Turn off the heat.

3. Remove the softened gelatine from the water and squeeze off the excess moisture. Discard the water.

154

4. Add the gelatine to the warm wine mixture and stir until completely melted. Allow to cool.

5. Divide the blackberries between 4 glasses. Carefully pour the cooled wine over the fruit and leave to set in the refridgerator for 3–4 hours or overnight. Garnish with the sprigs of mint and serve.

PASSIONFRUIT AND MUSCAT SYLLABUB

This is a very rich pudding that is enjoyed by children and adults alike. It is not a true syllabub, which is a rather more complicated pudding that was popular during the reign of Elizabeth I; nonetheless it is a quick and easy way to serve something of similar creaminess.

The passionfruit should be slightly wrinkly in appearance to ensure that the flesh will be sweet and juicy. It should not, however, be completely shrivelled – as this may mean that the fruit is just old and will be dry. Serve with ginger biscuits to make a more sophisticated pudding suitable for a dinner party.

Preparation time: 15 minutes
Serves 6

8 ripe passionfruits	*3 tablespoons Muscat wine*
250ml/9fl oz Mascarpone cheese	*2 tablespoons icing sugar*
200ml/7fl oz crème fraîche	*juice of 1 lemon*

1. Halve the passionfruits, scoop out the seeds and juice and set aside.

2. Mix together the Mascarpone, crème fraîche and Muscat. Sift in the icing sugar. Season to taste with the lemon juice. Fold in the passionfruit seeds and juice, reserving a few seeds for decoration.

3. Pour into stem glasses and decorate with the reserved seeds. Chill well before serving.

RHUBARB, ORANGE AND GINGERNUT PUDDING

This quick and easy pudding is ideal for early-summer supper parties. The ginger base is there to add an element of surprise and texture but of course it is optional – the rhubarb cream on its own makes for a good fool.

Preparation time: 15 minutes
Chilling time: 30 minutes
Serves 4–6

285g/10oz rhubarb, washed and
  cut into 2.5cm/1in slices
juice of 1 orange
55g/2oz caster sugar
10 gingernut biscuits, crushed

30g/1oz unsalted butter, melted
30g/1oz demerara sugar
grated zest of ½ orange
200ml/7fl oz double cream,
  lightly whipped

1. Place the rhubarb in a saucepan with the orange juice and the caster sugar and heat gently until the rhubarb is tender and cooked.
2. Mix together the ginger biscuits with the butter and demerara sugar. Press into the bottom of 4 ramekins.
3. Drain the rhubarb to remove any excess liquid. In a food processor or blender, or using a fork, mash the rhubarb to a rough purée. Stir in the orange zest and then fold in the cream.
4. Pour the mixture over the ginger biscuit base and allow to chill in the refridgerator.

SUMMER PUDDING

This recipe must be prepared a day in advance. It is the perfect dessert for a hot summer's day. It is important that stale bread is used; fresh bread produces rather a 'pappy' finish. Summer puddings can also be made in individual portions using metal timbales for the mould.

Preparation time: 30 minutes (plus overnight refrigeration)
Serves 6

900g/2lb mixed redcurrants,
blackcurrants, blackberries,
raspberries and strawberries (or
a selection of just some of these)
2 tablespoons water

170g/6oz caster sugar
6–9 slices stale white bread

To serve
double cream, lightly whipped

1. Cook the redcurrants, blackcurrants and blackberries with the water and sugar in a saucepan for 5 minutes, or until just soft but still bright in colour. Add the raspberries and strawberries. Drain off most of the juice and reserve.
2. Dip the slices of bread into the reserved fruit juice and use to line a pudding basin.
3. While the fruit is still just warm, pour it into the bread-lined basin. Cover with a rounded piece of bread dipped in the fruit juice. Tip the remaining juice into a saucepan and reduce by boiling to a syrupy consistency. Leave to cool.
4. Stand the pudding basin on a dish. Press a saucer or plate on top of the pudding and place a 450g/1lb weight on top. Leave in a cool place overnight.
5. Remove the saucer and weight. Invert a serving dish over the bowl and turn both over together. Give the bowl and plate a sharp shake and remove the bowl. Spoon the reserved, reduced fruit juice over the pudding. Serve the cream separately.

INSTANT CRÈME BRÛLÉE

This instant crème brûlée is quick and easy to make but fantastically rich. If it seems too rich for your taste, use a little plain or vanilla yoghurt in place of the Mascarpone. A very little water can be sprinkled over the sugar before carmelizing – it means that it will brûlée quickly.

Preparation and cooking time: 10 minutes
Serves 4

250g/9oz *Mascarpone cheese*   *icing sugar, to taste*
vanilla essence   *caster sugar*

1. Beat the Mascarpone cheese lightly. Add the vanilla essence and icing sugar to taste.
2. Divide the mixture between 4 ramekin dishes and spread flat. Chill in the fridge.
3. Sprinkle the top of the ramekins with a thin even layer of caster sugar.
4. Using a blow torch, first melt the sugar and then allow it to caramelise.
5. Leave to cool and harden before serving.

THAI RICE PUDDING

This is a simple rice pudding but the addition of lemon grass and cardamom makes it seem fairly exotic. Serve it with a fruit coulis such as mango and passionfruit.

If time allows, the flavour will improve if you first heat the milk and add the lemon grass and cardamom, remove from the heat and leave to infuse for 20 minutes. Then add the rice and sugar and follow the recipe.

Preparation time: 5 minutes
Cooking time: 25 minutes
Serves 4

110g/4oz *Thai jasmine rice*   To serve
570ml/1 pint milk   1 small carton *crème fraîche*
55g/2oz *caster sugar*   *(optional)*
1 piece lemon grass, *chopped*   *fruit coulis*
6 *whole cardamom pods, bruised*

1. Rinse the rice and put it into a saucepan with the milk and sugar. Tie up the cardamom and lemon grass in a clean J-cloth (not pink) or a piece of muslin and add it to the milk.
2. Bring slowly to the boil and simmer, stirring occasionally, for 25 minutes or until the mixture has thickened.
3. Remove the lemon grass and cardamom and serve with the fruit coulis and the crème fraîche, if using.

PEACH AND ALMOND COBBLER

A cobbler is a pudding that is put together quickly – or 'cobbled together'. This peach version is particularly popular in the southern states of America, where peaches are plentiful. However, any soft fruit can be substituted for the peaches in this easy recipe; plums, nectarines or apricots are particularly good.

To remove the skin from peaches, immerse the fruit in boiling water for 30 seconds, then remove to cold water. The skins should slip away easily with the help of a small knife.

Preparation time: 10 minutes
Cooking time: 20 minutes
Serves 4

6 ripe peaches
2 tablespoons caster sugar
large pinch of ground cinnamon
2 tablespoons cornflour

55g/2oz cold butter
2–3 tablespoons caster sugar
100ml/3½fl oz milk
1 tablespoon flaked almonds

For the topping
110g/4oz self-raising flour
pinch of salt

To serve
150ml/¼ pint double cream

1. Preheat the oven to 190°C/375°F/gas mark 5.
2. Peel the peaches. Cut into quarters, remove the stones and place in a bowl.
3. Mix together the sugar, cinnamon and cornflour. Add to the peaches. Mix well
4. Place the coated peaches in a single layer in a 20cm/8in ovenproof dish.

5. To make the topping, sift the flour with the salt into a large bowl or food processor.

6. Cut the butter into 1cm/½in cubes and toss into the flour. Using two knives or the food processor, cut in the butter until the mixture resembles very coarse breadcrumbs. Tip into a bowl if using a food processor. Stir in the sugar.

7. Quickly stir in the milk. The mixture will become very sticky.

8. Using a teaspoon, dot the cobbler mixture over the fruit. Sprinkle with the almonds.

9. Bake in the top third of the oven for 20 minutes or until the fruit is soft when pierced with a skewer and the topping is pale brown.

10. Serve warm with cream.

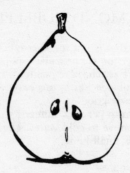

PEAR AND ALMOND TART

This recipe could not be easier – the margin will rise to give the tart natural sides. It is important that the pears are good and ripe. Serve with plenty of ice cream.

Preparation time: 20 minutes
Cooking time: 20 minutes
Serves 4

1 sheet puff pastry (30cm/12in × 21cm/8in)
1 tablespoon caster sugar
2 tablespoons ground almonds
30g/1oz butter
2 ripe pears

30g/1oz flaked almonds
2 tablespoons runny honey

To serve
vanilla ice cream

1. Preheat the oven to 200°C/400°F/gas mark 6.
2. Lay the sheet of pastry on a baking sheet and prick it all over with a fork, leaving a 2.5cm/1in margin around the edge.
3. Sprinkle the caster sugar and ground almonds on to the base, being careful not to go over the margin.
4. Cut up the butter and dot it over the ground almonds and caster sugar.
5. Slice the pears and lay them over the pastry – again, leaving the margin clear.
6. Sprinkle the pears with the flaked almonds and drizzle the honey over the top.
7. Bake in the top third of the oven for 20–25 minutes.

RHUBARB SPONGE

This delicious sponge cake can be served as a teatime cake or as a pudding with plenty of custard. If you are serving it as a pudding, it can be removed from the oven after 50 minutes when it will still be just moist in the centre. Serve warm.

Preparation time: 30 minutes
Cooking time: 50–60 minutes
Serves 6–8

340g/12oz rhubarb, cut into
* 2.5cm/1in pieces*
finely grated zest of 2 oranges
225g/8oz caster sugar

170g/6oz unsalted butter, plus
* extra for greasing*
½ teaspoon vanilla extract
3 eggs, separated
225g/8oz self-raising flour, sifted

1. Place the rhubarb, orange zest and 2 tablespoons of the sugar into a saucepan. Cook, covered, for 5–7 minutes, or until just soft but still holding its shape.
2. Strain, reserving the syrup, and allow to cool.
3. Preheat the oven to 180°C/350°F/gas mark 4. Grease a 22.5cm/9in cake tin and line with a disc of greased greaseproof paper.
4. Cream together the butter and remaining sugar in a large bowl until light and fluffy. Beat in the vanilla extract.
5. Gradually add the egg yolks to the creamed mixture, beating well between each addition, then fold in the flour. Stir in the drained, cooled

rhubarb. It will break up a little bit, but this is normal.

6. In a separate bowl, whisk the egg whites until medium peaks are formed. Carefully fold the egg whites into the creamed mixture. The mixture will be quite stiff at this stage.

7. Turn the mixture into the prepared cake tin and bake in the centre of the preheated oven for 50–60 minutes or until lightly browned and well risen and a skewer inserted into the centre comes out clean.

8. Meanwhile, put the reserved syrup into a small saucepan and boil rapidly until reduced by a third. With a skewer, pierce the surface of the cake all over. Pour the hot syrup over the cake. Allow to cool in the tin before turning out on to a wire rack and allowing it to cool completely.

BAKED PEACHES WITH STRAWBERRY CREAM

This clean and refreshing, simple summer pudding can be prepared in advance and then baked at the last minute. However, do not hull strawberries more than 2–3 hours ahead of time, in order that they do not soften too much.

Preparation time: 15 minutes
Cooking time: 20 minutes
Serves 4

*150ml/¼ pint double cream,
    lightly whipped*
*140g/5oz ripe strawberries, hulled
    and chopped*
4 ripe peaches
*2 tablespoons Amaretto, or
    orange juice if preferred*

soft brown sugar
*6 Amaretti biscuits, roughly
    crushed*

To garnish
fresh strawberries

1. Preheat the oven to 180°C/350°F/gas mark 4.

2. Gently stir together the strawberries and double cream.

3. Cut the peaches in half lengthways and remove the stones. Place in a shallow ovenproof dish and sprinkle the Amaretto and soft brown sugar over the top.

4. Place in the oven for 10 minutes or until just beginning to 'give'. Stir the Amaretti biscuits into the strawberry cream.

5. Place two peach halves on each of 4 plates. Drizzle a little of the juices from the bottom of the pan over the peaches, then place a large spoonful of the cream on the top or to the side. Garnish with a few fresh strawberries.

SUMMER FRUIT ALASKA

These delicious puddings are quick and easy to prepare and will give your guests a wonderful surprise. They are ideal for a summer evening. They are very sweet, so it is a good idea to serve them with a biscuit or shortbread. It is important to use good-quality ice cream; the cheaper varieties have more air in them and are more likely to melt in the heat of the oven.

Preparation time: 10 minutes
Cooking time: 5 minutes
Serves 6

6 generous scoops good-quality
   vanilla ice cream
340g/12oz mixed summer berries
   (for example, raspberries,
   blueberries, strawberries)

2 tablespoons crème de cassis
icing sugar to taste
2 egg whites
110g/4oz caster sugar, plus a little
   extra for dusting

1. Place the ice-cream scoops on a baking sheet and put into the freezer until completely solid.
2. Meanwhile, prepare the soft fruit: wash as necessary and hull and halve the strawberries if using.
3. Divide the fruit between 6 ramekins. Add the crème de cassis and sprinkle with a little icing sugar if the fruit is tart.
4. Preheat the oven to 230°C/450°F/gas mark 6.
5. Whisk the egg whites with a pinch of salt until stiff but not dry.
6. Add half of sugar and whisk again until very stiff and shiny. Fold in the remaining sugar.
7. Place a scoop of the ice cream on top of each fruit compote. Divide the meringue between the ramekins, creating a dome over each one; ensure that the meringue reaches the edges of the ramekin so that the fruit cannot be seen. Dust each one lightly with a little extra caster sugar.
8. Place the ramekins on a baking sheet and bake in the preheated oven for 3–5 minutes until golden brown on the top. Serve immediately.

RASPBERRY AND ALMOND CREAMS

This is a dinner-party pudding that can be prepared several hours in advance. Mascarpone is a very useful ingredient – it makes the 'cream' taste rather like an elegant cheesecake. The use of blackcurrant cordial is with children in mind; if you are making the pudding just for adults, use crème de cassis instead.

Preparation time: 15 minutes
Serves 4

340g/¾lb frozen summer berries,
  defrosted
2 tablespoons icing sugar
2 teaspoons blackcurrant cordial
140g/5oz Mascarpone cheese

140g/5oz Greek yoghurt
1 × 125g/4½oz punnet fresh
  raspberries
16 Amaretti biscuits, roughly
  crushed

1. Push the defrosted summer berries through a sieve and stir in the icing sugar and blackcurrant cordial or crème de cassis.
2. Beat together the Mascarpone and Greek yoghurt in a bowl and swirl in 1 tablespoon of the fruit sauce to create a marbled effect.
3. Put 2 tablespoons of the cream mixture into each of 4 tall glasses. Top with 2 tablespoons of the fruit sauce, some fresh raspberries and sprinkle with some of the Amaretti biscuits. Repeat the layers until all the cream and fruit mixture are used up, finishing with a few fresh raspberries. Chill before serving.

INDIVIDUAL CHOCOLATE MOUSSE CAKE WITH RED BERRIES

The mousse cake can be made a day in advance – and in fact its texture will improve overnight – but should not be cut into rounds until you are ready to assemble the puddings. The recipe calls for fruit coulis – this can be made by whizzing together defrosted raspberries with a little icing sugar and pushing the mixture through a sieve. Alternatively, fruit coulis are available in most supermarkets.

Preparation time: 15 minutes
Cooking time: 12 minutes
Presentation time: 10 minutes
Serves 6

225g/8oz plain chocolate, roughly
   chopped
85ml/3fl oz water
1 teaspoon strong instant coffee
   powder
5 eggs
140g/5oz caster sugar

200ml/7 fl oz double cream,
   lightly whipped
fresh fruit (for example,
   raspberries)

To garnish
icing sugar
fruit coulis
mint sprigs

1. Line a large roasting pan (approx 30cm/12in × 22cm/9in) with silicone paper. Preheat the oven to 200°C/400°F/gas mark 6.
2. Put the chocolate, water and coffee into a heavy saucepan over a low heat. When melted, remove from the heat and allow to cool slightly.
3. Separate the eggs and beat together the yolks and the caster sugar until pale and mousse-like.
4. Whisk the whites until stiff but not dry. Add the melted chocolate to the egg and caster sugar mixture.
5. With a large metal spoon, stir a small amount of the whisked egg white thoroughly into the chocolate mixture to loosen it. Fold the remaining whites in gently. Spread the mixture evenly on to the baking parchment.
6. Bake in the preheated oven for about 12 minutes, until the top is slightly browned and firm to the touch.
7. Slide the cake and parchment out of the roasting pan on to a wire rack. Cover immediately with a damp teatowel (to prevent the cake from cracking) and leave to cool.
8. When the cake is cool, use a pastry cutter to cut it into 12 rounds.
9. To assemble: spread the whipped cream over 6 of the cake circles and arrange the fruit on the top. Put 1 dressed circle on to each of 6 plates. Place a second round of cake on top of each. Dust heavily with icing sugar and pour fruit coulis around the edge of the plates, then garnish with a small pile of the fresh fruit and a mint sprig.

PASSION PUDDING

These delicious puddings are best made a day in advance; by the time they are eaten, the soft dark brown sugar will have partly dissolved into a delicious molass at the bottom of each ramekin dish. For variety a few seedless grapes can be placed in the bottom of each ramekin before the pudding mixture is added.

Preparation time: 5 minutes
Serves 4

150ml/¼ pint double cream
150ml/¼ pint natural yoghurt
soft dark brown sugar

1. Whip the cream until it just holds its shape. Add the yoghurt and whip until soft peaks are formed.
2. Divide the mixture between 4 ramekin dishes and sprinkle approximately 6mm/¼ in of soft brown sugar over the top of each one. (The puddings should be completely covered with sugar.)
3. Leave in the refridgerator overnight or for at least 1 hour.

HONEY BAVAROIS

For this recipe we recommend the use of leaf gelatine, which is now widely available in most good supermarkets, is remarkably easy to use and is much more foolproof than the powdered versions. Dishes made using gelatine are unsuitable for freezing and for vegetarian diets. Serve with a fruit salad or fruit coulis. Coulis can be made by blending soft fruits such as raspberries with a little icing sugar until smooth; push through a sieve and chill until ready to serve.

Preparation time: 30 minutes
Serves 4

340ml/12fl oz milk
30ml/2 tablespoons honey
4 large egg yolks
110g/4oz caster sugar
2½ leaves gelatine

250ml/½ pint double cream,
  lightly whipped

To serve
fruit coulis or fruit salad

1. In a heavy-based pan, warm the milk and honey.
2. Beat together the egg yolks and sugar in a bowl. Pour the milk and honey on to the egg yolks, stirring steadily. Wash the pan and return the milk and egg mixture to it.
3. Over a low heat, stir the milk mixture until it begins to thicken and will coat the back of a spoon. Strain into a bowl. Meanwhile, soak the gelatine according to the manufacturer's instructions.

4. Add the gelatine to the hot custard and stir until the gelatine is incorporated. Place the bowl in a large shallow bowl of cold water for 10 minutes; when the mixture is on the point of setting, fold in the cream. Turn into a terrine mould or a plastic box lined with clingfilm and place in the fridge to set.
5. Turn out and serve with the fruit coulis or fruit salad.

SUMMER FRUIT KEBABS

The lime in these fruit kebabs makes them particularly delicious. They can also be cooked on the barbecue or on a griddle. Soak the wooden skewers in water for 30 minutes before threading on the fruit so that they don't burst into flames when placed over (or under) the heat.

Preparation and macerating time: 45 minutes
Cooking time: 10 minutes
Serves 4

zest and juice of ½ a lime
1 tablespoon Cointreau
1 tablespoon runny honey
¼ pineapple, cut into 2.5cm/1in cubes
2 bananas, cut into 1.25cm/½in slices

2 peaches, stoned and cut into chunks

To serve
crème fraîche or vanilla ice cream

1. Mix together the lime juice, Cointreau and honey.
2. Drizzle the mixture over the fruit and leave to macerate for 30 minutes.
3. Preheat the grill to its highest temperature.
4. Thread the fruit on to wooden skewers and place the kebabs under the grill, basting with the juices occasionally.
5. Serve immediately with the crème fraîche or ice cream.

CHOCOLATE TART

The success of this very rich chocolate tart depends mainly on the quality of the chocolate – try to buy one that is at least 70 per cent cocoa solids. It is important to add the Kalhua with or after the cream – alcohol can make the chocolate seize up into a solid mass if the instructions are not followed. We have suggested buying a ready-baked shortcrust pastry case for convenience, but if you have the time home-made pastry is far superior. For this recipe you will need 225g/8oz flour-quantity shortcrust pastry.

Preparation time: 5 minutes
Chilling time: 2–3 hours
Serves 6

225g/8oz good-quality dark
   chocolate
290ml/½ pint cream
3 tablespoons Kalhua
1 × 20cm/8in sweet shortcrust
   ready-baked pastry case
icing sugar

few drops coffee essence

To serve
fresh fruit

To garnish
chocolate shavings

1. Melt the chocolate with half the cream and the Kalhua. Pour into the pre-baked pastry case and leave in the refridgerator for 2–3 hours.
2. Just before serving, whip the rest of the cream with the coffee essence. Add the icing sugar to taste and pile the mixture into a bowl.
3. Sprinkle the chocolate shavings over the top of the tart. Serve a slice of the tart with the coffee-flavoured cream and fresh fruit.

BANANA AND BUTTERSCOTCH PUFF-PASTRY TARTS

These delicious tarts are quick and simple to prepare, look very professional and are popular with adults and children alike. As the pastry cooks, it rises up around the bananas.

Preparation time: 10 minutes
Cooking time: 20 minutes
Serves 4

2 tablespoons brandy
110g/4oz unsalted butter,
  chopped
55g/2oz demerara sugar
2 tablespoons double cream

1 pack puff pastry
3 medium-sized bananas

To serve
crème fraîche

1. Preheat the oven to 200°C/400°F/gas mark 6.
2. Make the butterscotch sauce: place the brandy, butter, sugar and double cream in a small saucepan. Heat until the butter has melted and all the ingredients have combined to make a smooth sauce. Set aside to cool completely.
3. Roll the puff pastry into 4 × 15cm/6in squares the thickness of a 20p coin.
4. Place the pastry squares on a baking sheet.
5. Peel the bananas and cut on the diagonal into 1cm/½in slices. Mix with 4 tablespoons of the butterscotch sauce.
6. Pile the bananas on to the squares, leaving a ½ cm/¼in border all the way round.
7. Bake on the top shelf of the preheated oven for 15–20 minutes or until brown and well risen.
8. Serve immediately with the remaining sauce and a spoonful of crème fraîche.

COCONUT ICE CREAM

This delicious firm ice cream is particularly good if served with chocolate sauce – ideal for Bounty lovers. If desired a little alcohol can be added just prior to freezing – 1 or 2 tablespoons of Malibu, for example, gives a more exotic flavour.

Preparation time: 15 minutes (plus freezing time)
Serves 4

290ml/½ pint double cream   55g/2oz caster sugar
290ml/½ pint thick coconut milk   4 egg yolks
55g/2oz desiccated coconut

1. Bring the cream, coconut milk and desiccated coconut to the boil in a large heavy saucepan. Remove from the heat, cover and set aside for 30 minutes to infuse.
2. In a large bowl, whisk the caster sugar with the egg yolks until creamy. Add the coconut infusion and gradually mix together.
3. Return the mixture to the pan and cook over a low heat, stirring constantly with a wooden spoon, until the custard is thick enough to coat the back of a spoon. Take care not to overheat and scramble the eggs. Leave to cool.
4. Pour the mixture into a tray and freeze.
5. When the mixture is half-frozen, remove from the freezer and whisk again. Return to the freezer.

LEMON ICE CREAM

This must be the easiest recipe we have ever written – and it is sensationally delicious as long as you use very good-quality lemon curd. It tastes better than any ready-made lemon ice cream we have ever eaten.

Preparation time: 3 minutes
Freezing time: 1 hour
Serves 4

1 good-quality jar lemon curd
570ml/1 pint double cream

1. Mix together the lemon curd and the double cream. Tip into a plastic freezer container and freeze until firm.
2. Serve with ginger shortbread.

CHRISTMAS CAKE AND MADEIRA ICE CREAM

This recipe is for leftover Christmas cake. It is delicious but fantastically rich, so serve it after a light main course. We would suggest making double the quantity and freezing it in 2 containers.

Preparation time: 5 minutes
Cooking time: 10 minutes
Serves 6

170g/6oz Christmas or other
  fruitcake
5 tablespoons Madeira
570ml/1 pint double cream
1 vanilla pod, split
5 egg yolks
110g/4oz soft light brown sugar

1. Roughly crumble the fruitcake into a small bowl and cover with the Madeira. Leave to soak for 10 minutes.
2. Meanwhile, put the cream and the vanilla pod into a small saucepan and bring to the boil.
3. Beat the egg yolks and sugar together and pour over the custard mixture to the rinsed-out pan and cook over a gentle heat, stirring continuously, until the mixture thickens and coats the back of a wooden spoon. Strain into a clean bowl and allow to cool.
4. When completely cold, stir the fruitcake into the custard and transfer to a shallow freezeproof tray and freeze for 30–45 minutes. Remove from the freezer and beat the mixture to break down any large ice crystals. Return to the freezer for a further 45–60 minutes or until completely frozen.

CAKES AND BISCUITS

AMERICAN CARROT CAKE

Carrot cake, sometimes known as passion cake, is an American classic. It is an excellent choice for those trying to keep their cholesterol under control, because it uses oil instead of butter. It improves if kept for a day or two before serving. The carrots and pineapple keep it extra moist so it can be stored well for up to 5 days, although it will probably disappear long before then! It can also be frozen for up to 1 month. It can be made quickly in the food processor.

Preparation time: 15 minutes
Cooking time: 45 minutes

2 medium eggs
225g/8oz caster sugar
170 ml/6fl oz sunflower or
  vegetable oil
½ teaspoon vanilla essence
140g/5oz tinned pineapples,
  drained and finely chopped
140g/5oz carrots, grated

170g/6oz self-raising flour
pinch of salt
1 teaspoon ground mixed spice
½ teaspoon ground cinnamon
100g/3½oz chopped walnuts
1 tablespoon icing sugar for
  dusting

1. Prepare a deep 20cm/8in cake tin by brushing with a little of the oil and lining the base with a disc of greaseproof paper.
2. Preheat the oven to 180°C/350°F/gas mark 4.
3. Beat the eggs with the caster sugar, then stir in the oil, vanilla, pineapple and carrots.
4. Sieve together the flour, salt and spices. Fold into the carrot mixture.
5. Fold in the walnuts, then turn the mixture into the prepared tin.
6. Bake in the centre of the preheated oven until the cake is risen and

golden. This should take about 45 minutes – it is ready when it springs back if pressed lightly in the centre.

7. Cool on a wire rack. To serve, dust with the icing sugar.

PEAR AND VANILLA UPSIDE-DOWN CAKE

This recipe calls for the seeds of a vanilla pod: simply split the pod lengthways with a sharp knife and remove the seeds with a teaspoon. If this seems too extravagant, use vanilla sugar. To make vanilla sugar, fill a large jar with caster sugar, press in a vanilla pod and leave overnight. Use the sugar as required and replace with more plain sugar – in this way you can keep a vanilla pod for months.

Preparation time: 20–25 minutes
Cooking time: 40 minutes

85g/3oz butter, softened
85g/3oz sugar
2 eggs, beaten
seeds of 1 vanilla pod
85g/3oz self-raising flour, sifted
milk, if necessary

For the topping
30g/1oz butter
55g/2oz caster sugar
2 ripe pears, peeled, quartered
*   and cored*

To serve
crème fraîche or ice cream

1. Preheat the oven to 180°C/350°F/gas mark 4.

2. Spread the butter around the base and sides of a 20cm/8in cake tin. Sprinkle with the caster sugar.

3. Slice each pear quarter and arrange the slices over the base of the tin. Set aside.

4. In a large bowl, beat the butter, sugar and vanilla seeds together until light and fluffy. Beat in the eggs, a little at a time, adding a spoonful of flour if the mixture looks about to curdle.

5. Sift in the flour and mix in gently, adding a little milk or water if necessary, until the mixture is of a soft, dropping consistency.

6. Carefully spoon the mixture over the pears and level the surface.

7. Bake the sponge in the centre of the preheated oven for 30–45 minutes or until well risen and golden brown. Allow to cool slightly in the tin before carefully turning out on to a serving plate. Serve warm with crème fraîche or ice cream.

DEVIL'S FOOD CAKE

There are many fables about how this dark chocolate cake earned its name. Perhaps it conjures up thoughts of the Devil because it is sinfully rich and decadent? What is certain is that it is a firm favourite of chocoholics and small children alike.

The cake is very moist so it keeps well for up to 3 days. It can also be frozen, complete with icing, for up to 1 month, so it is the ideal 'make-ahead' cake for special occasions. Open-freeze, then wrap closely with a double layer of clingfilm.

Preparation time: 40 minutes (including icing)
Cooking time: 25 minutes

85g/3oz good-quality plain chocolate, finely chopped
1 tablespoon cocoa powder
200 ml/7fl oz boiling water
140g/5oz plain flour
1 scant teaspoon bicarbonate of soda
140g/5oz butter, softened
170g/6oz light brown sugar
2 medium eggs, beaten

2 tablespoons crème fraîche
½ teaspoon vanilla extract

For the icing
110g/4oz plain chocolate, finely chopped
2 tablespoons cocoa powder
55ml/2fl oz water
55g/2oz butter, softened
1 tablespoon crème fraîche
170g/6oz icing sugar, sifted

1. Preheat the oven to 180°C/350°F/gas mark 4. Prepare two 20cm/8in shallow cake tins by greasing with a little soft butter and lining the bases with baking parchment.
2. To make the cake: place the chocolate and the cocoa in a bowl and add the boiling water. Stir to combine and melt the chocolate. Allow to cool to room temperature.
3. Sieve together the flour and the bicarbonate of soda. Set aside.
4. Beat the butter and the sugar until light, about 3 minutes. Add the eggs gradually while beating.
5. Stir in the crème fraîche and the vanilla.
6. Working quickly, stir in a third of the chocolate mixture, then a third of the flour. Continue adding the chocolate and the flour until the cake is mixed.

7. Divide the mixture equally between the two prepared tins, smoothing the surface to the edges of the tins.

8. Bake in the centre of the preheated oven for 20–25 minutes. When done, the cakes will be well risen and will spring back if touched lightly in the centre; a skewer inserted in the centre will come out clean.

9. Allow to cool in the tins for 20 minutes, then turn out on to a wire rack to finish cooling. Peel off the parchment paper.

10. For the icing: place the chocolate, cocoa and water in a small saucepan and heat over a low heat, stirring, until the chocolate is melted. Allow to cool to room temperature.

11. Beat the butter into the chocolate a little at a time. Stir in the crème fraîche.

12. Stir in the icing sugar, then use the icing to sandwich the two cakes together and to cover the sides and top. If the icing is very soft, place the cake in the refridgerator for about 10 minutes before serving.

CHOCOLATE AND ORANGE FAIRY CAKES

This quantity makes 24 deliciously light cakes that are perfect for tea. They freeze well, but should not be iced until they have been defrosted.

Preparation time: 15 minutes
Cooking time: 25–30 minutes
Makes 12 orange and 12 chocolate cakes

170g/6oz butter
170g/6oz caster sugar
3 eggs
170g/6oz self-raising flour
85g/3oz chocolate drops
zest and juice of 2 oranges

For the orange icing
110g/4oz icing sugar, sifted
zest and juice of one orange

For the chocolate icing
55g/2oz chocolate, chopped
1½ tablespoons golden syrup
½ tablespoon water
15g/½oz butter

1. Preheat the oven to 190°C/375°F/gas mark 5.
2. Prepare 2 × 12-hole bun tins by putting a paper case into each mould.

3. Cream together the butter and sugar until light and fluffy.

4. In a separate bowl, mix together the eggs, then gradually beat them into the creamed mixture, a little at a time, adding 1 tablespoon of flour if the mixture begins to curdle. Stir in the chocolate and orange zest.

5. Fold in the flour, adding orange juice to bring the mixture to a dropping consistency.

6. Divide the mixture between the cases so that each is ⅔ full.

7. Bake in the centre of the preheated oven for about 20 minutes, or until the cakes are well risen, golden and feel spongy to the fingertips. Allow to cool on a wire rack.

8. Make the icings. Orange: place the icing sugar and orange zest into a bowl, add enough orange juice to mix to a fairly stiff consistency. The icing should hold a trail when dropped from a spoon but gradually find its own level. It needs surprisingly little liquid. Chocolate: melt together all the ingredients over a low heat.

9. Ice half the cakes with the orange icing and half with the chocolate icing.

HONEY AND SESAME SEED BISCUITS

When this recipe was tested at Leith's we could hardly wait for the biscuits to cool and harden before we ate them. They can be served as a sweet biscuit but they are also delicious served with cheese.

Preparation time: 25 minutes
Cooking time: 35 minutes
Makes 18 biscuits

225g/8oz plain wholemeal flour	2 tablespoons sesame seeds
½ teaspoon salt	2 tablespoons runny honey
110g/4oz butter, diced	flour for rolling and dusting

1. Preheat the oven to 190°C/375°F/gas mark 5. Dust two baking sheets lightly with flour.

2. Sift the flour and salt into a large bowl and rub in the butter until the mixture resembles coarse breadcrumbs.

3. Stir in the sesame seeds and honey and bind together to a dough.

4. Turn the mixture on to a floured surface and knead lightly. Roll the mixture to the thickness of a £1 coin. Using a 5cm/2in plain or fluted cutter, stamp the rolled-out mixture into 18 rounds.

5. Transfer the biscuits to the prepared baking sheets and bake in the centre of the preheated oven for 35 minutes or until crisp, dry and brown. Transfer to a wire rack to cool. Store in an airtight container.

PEANUT BUTTER COOKIES

These biscuits are fairly quick to make and are very popular with children. They can be eaten for tea but are also delicious served with ice cream. The raw dough can be frozen in balls and then baked as required. Once baked, the biscuits will keep in an airtight container for up to 5 days.

Preparation time: 10 minutes
Cooking time: 15 minutes
Makes about 40 biscuits

140g/5oz butter
110g/4oz caster sugar
110g/4oz soft light brown sugar
1 large egg, beaten
110g/4oz crunchy peanut butter

½ teaspoon vanilla essence
200g/7oz plain flour
½ teaspoon salt
1 teaspoon baking powder

1. Preheat the oven to 180°C/350°F/gas mark 4.
2. Cream together the butter and both sugars until smooth and soft. Beat in the egg, then the peanut butter, and then add the vanilla essence.
3. Sift the flour with the salt and the baking powder into the mixture and stir until smooth. Do not overbeat or the dough will become oily.
4. Using your fingers, roll the mixture into about 40 small balls. Place well apart on 3 ungreased baking sheets and flatten with the tines of a fork.
5. Bake in the preheated oven for 10–15 minutes to an even (not too dark) brown.
6. While the biscuits are hot, ease them away from the baking sheets with a palette knife or fish slice and cool on a wire rack. Once completely cold and crisp, store in an airtight container.

LEMON AND POPPY SEED BISCUITS

These biscuits have a delicious clean, fresh flavour. They can be served with tea or coffee as an accompaniment for puddings. They are particularly good with ginger ice cream.

Preparation time: 15 minutes
Cooking time: 10 minutes
Makes 22 biscuits

110g/4oz butter, softened	*225g/8oz plain flour, sifted*
110g/4oz soft light brown sugar	*pinch of salt*
1 egg, beaten	*30g/1oz semolina*
finely grated zest of 2 lemons	*icing sugar*
45g/1½oz poppy seeds	*flour for dusting and rolling*

1. Preheat the oven to 190°C/375°F/gas mark 5. Dust 2 baking sheets lightly with flour.
2. In a large bowl, beat together the butter and sugar until creamy. Beat in the egg a little at a time.
3. Stir in the lemon zest and poppy seeds.
4. Mix in the flour, salt and semolina to form a stiffish paste, then turn the mixture out on to a floured surface.
5. Roll the paste to the thickness of a £1 coin. Using a 5cm/2in plain or fluted cutter, stamp the rolled-out mixture into 22 rounds.
6. Place the biscuits on the prepared baking sheets and chill for 10 minutes. Bake in the centre of the preheated oven for 20 minutes or until set and lightly browned.
7. Transfer to a cooling rack and dust with icing sugar when cold.
8. Store in an airtight container.

APPLE AND CINNAMON COOKIES

This recipe makes plenty of cookies. They can be baked in batches (ideally they should be cooked in the centre of the oven), and once cool they can be frozen – they won't keep for more than a day or two after baking. Serve as a coffee or teatime treat. If you don't have fresh apple, dried apple pieces are a good substitute.

Preparation time: 10 minutes
Cooking time: 10–15 minutes
Makes 24–30

butter for greasing
110g/4oz unsalted butter
170g/6oz caster sugar
1 egg, beaten
½ tablespoon lemon juice
grated zest of 1 lemon
4 teaspoons cinnamon

200g/7oz plain flour
1 teaspoon baking powder
pinch of salt
200g/7oz dessert apple, peeled
*   and chopped into small cubes*
icing sugar

1. Preheat the oven to 190°C/375°F/gas mark 5. Grease 3 baking sheets with butter.
2. Cream together the butter and sugar until pale and fluffy.
3. Add the egg gradually, beating well between each addition. Add the lemon juice and zest and mix well.
4. Sift in the flour, cinnamon, baking powder and salt and mix to a stiffish dough. Stir in the chopped apple.
5. Place large spoonfuls of the mixture on each tray – leave room for the biscuits to spread.
6. Bake in the centre of the preheated oven for 10–15 minutes until golden brown. Leave to cool on a wire rack.
7. Before serving, dust with a little icing sugar and, if desired, a little more cinnamon.

BANANA, MILK CHOCOLATE AND PECAN BISCUITS

Preparation time: 15 minutes
Cooking time: 25 minutes
Makes 20

110g/4oz butter
55g/2oz soft light brown sugar
2 bananas

85g/3oz pecan nuts
110g/4oz milk chocolate, broken
225g/8oz self-raising flour, sifted

1. Preheat the oven to 180°C/350°F/gas mark 4. Line 2 baking sheets with silicone paper.

2. Cream together the butter and sugar in a medium-sized bowl until light and fluffy.
3. Mash one of the bananas and dice the other. Chop the pecan nuts and chocolate roughly.
4. Beat the mashed banana into the creamed butter and sugar mixture. Stir in the diced banana, pecan nuts and chocolate.
5. Add the flour gradually. It will be difficult to begin with but will gradually become softish in texture – do not be tempted to add liquid.
6. Divide the mixture into 20 large pieces and arrange on the baking sheets at least 5cm/2in apart. Flatten very slightly.
7. Bake in the centre of the preheated oven for 20–25 minutes or until dry to the touch. Cool on a wire rack.

CHOCOLATE CHIP AND HAZELNUT COOKIES

These delicious biscuits can be made in advance and the raw dough can be frozen and baked when required. Once baked, they will keep in an airtight container for up to a week but they do not freeze very well.

Preparation time: 20 minutes
Cooking time: 15–20 minutes
Makes 18

110g/4oz butter
110g/4oz caster sugar
1 egg, beaten
170g/6oz plain flour, sifted
pinch of salt

1 teaspoon vanilla essence
110g/4oz dark chocolate, broken
55g/2oz hazelnuts, roughly
  chopped (optional)

1. Preheat the oven to 180°C/350°F/gas mark 4. Grease a baking sheet.
2. In a large bowl, cream the butter until soft, add the sugar and beat again until light and fluffy. Beat in the egg, the sifted flour, salt, vanilla essence, chocolate and nuts. Do not over-stir.
3. Place large teaspoonfuls of the mixture on to the prepared baking sheet and bake in the preheated oven for 10–12 minutes until golden brown and cooked through. Leave to cool on a wire rack.
4. Once completely cold and crisp, store in an airtight container.

MOCHA COOKIES

These biscuits are simple to make – when creaming the butter the trick is to place the bowl on a J-cloth; this will keep the bowl still and make beating easier. To melt the chocolate, break it into evenly sized pieces, place over, not in, a pan of simmering water. Stir occasionally until completely melted and then remove from the heat.

Preparation time: 25–30 minutes
Cooking time: 15–20 minutes
Makes 22

140g/5oz butter, softened
85g/3oz caster sugar
55g/2oz soft light brown sugar
1 medium egg, beaten
85g/3oz dark chocolate chips
½ teaspoon vanilla essence
140g/5oz plain flour

½ teaspoon salt
2 tablespoons cocoa powder
2 tablespoons finely ground fresh coffee
½ teaspoon baking powder
110g/4oz white chocolate, melted

1. Preheat the oven to 180°C/350°F/gas mark 4.
2. Cream the butter until soft. Add both the sugars and beat again until smooth and soft. Beat in the egg, then the chocolate chips and the vanilla essence.
3. Sift the dry ingredients on to the mixture and stir until smooth. Do not over-stir or the dough will become very oily.
4. Place spoonfuls, well apart, on 3 ungreased baking sheets. Flatten with the tines of a fork, and bake in the preheated oven for 10–15 minutes to an even (not too dark) brown.
5. While the biscuits are still hot, ease them from the baking sheets with a

palette knife or fish slice and leave to cool on a wire rack. Drizzle with the melted white chocolate. Once completely cold and crisp, store in an airtight container.

FIG, ALMOND AND CRÈME FRAÎCHE BISCUITS

These fig biscuits are particularly good served with hot black coffee after dinner. They are rich and intense but the use of crème fraîche makes for a particularly crumbly texture. The raw dough can be frozen, and the baked biscuits can be kept in an airtight container for 2–3 days.

Preparation time: 10 minutes
Cooking time: 30 minutes
Makes 16

110g/4oz soft light brown sugar
55g/2oz softened butter, diced
55g/2oz crème fraîche
110g/4oz plain flour, sifted, plus extra for rolling

55g/2oz ground almonds
85g/3oz dried figs, cut into large pieces
30g/1oz flaked almonds
icing sugar for dusting

1. Preheat the oven to 180°C/350°F/gas mark 4. Line 2 baking sheets with silicone paper.
2. Put all of the ingredients except for the flaked almonds and icing sugar into the bowl of a food processor and, using the pulse button, process for 15–20 seconds or until the mixture comes together to form a ball.
3. Turn the mixture on to a floured surface and divide into 16 portions. Roll each piece into a ball and flatten slightly with the palm of your hand or the back of a fork. Transfer to the baking sheets.
4. Sprinkle the flaked almonds over the biscuits and bake in the centre of the preheated oven for 30 minutes or until dry to the touch and lightly browned.
5. Allow to cool slightly, then remove to a wire rack to cool completely. Dust with icing sugar.

VIENNESE BISCUITS

These are classic biscuits that can be served plain or dipped in chocolate – simply melt 110g/4oz chopped plain chocolate with 30g/1oz butter in a bowl over, not in, a pan of simmering water.

Traditionally Viennese biscuits are piped on to the baking sheet using a medium-sized star nozzle. If you haven't a bag and nozzle, simply shape them into long thin biscuits.

Preparation time: 20 minutes
Cooking time: 15 minutes
Makes 24

butter for greasing
125g/4½oz unsalted butter
30g/1oz icing sugar

125g/4½oz plain flour
¼ teaspoon baking powder
few drops vanilla essence

1. Preheat the oven to 190°C/375°F/gas mark 5. Lightly grease 3 baking sheets.
2. Beat the butter until soft. Add the sifted icing sugar and beat again until light and fluffy.
3. Add the sifted flour, baking powder and vanilla essence, using your hands to work to a paste.
4. Pipe or shape into 24 biscuits and bake for 15 minutes in the preheated oven. Leave to cool on a wire rack.

MACADAMIA NUT BROWNIES

Everyone seems to like brownies, and these ones are particularly delicious – the smell in the kitchen as they bake is wonderful. Brownies can be chewy, cakey or fudgy depending on how much sugar is added. Whatever type of brownies are being made, the most important thing is not to overcook them. Test them by inserting a skewer into the centre of the brownies: there should be a little undercooked mixture on the skewer – they will firm up as they cool, and are better undercooked than overcooked.

183

Macadamia nuts are delicious but if you have difficulty finding them you can use hazelnuts or almonds instead, or indeed leave them out completely. The rum can also be omitted and replaced with milk. The brownies can be kept in the refridgerator for 2–3 days or frozen for up to 3 months.

Preparation time: 15 minutes
Cooking time: 30 minutes

melted lard or oil for greasing
110g/4oz unsalted butter
110g/4oz plain chocolate
2 eggs
170g/6oz caster sugar

55ml/2fl oz dark rum
110g/4oz plain flour
110g/4oz macadamia nuts,
  chopped

1. Preheat the oven to 180°C/350°F/gas mark 4. Grease a 20cm/8in shallow square tin and line with a piece of greased greaseproof paper.
2. Melt the butter and chocolate in a saucepan over a low heat without allowing to get too hot. Remove and allow to cool.
3. Beat the eggs and sugar together until light and thick. Stir in the cooled chocolate mixture and the rum.
4. Sift the flour and add to the mixture with the macadamia nuts. Fold in carefully and thoroughly, using a large metal spoon. Pile into the prepared tin.
5. Bake in the centre of the preheated oven for 30 minutes or until the centre of the brownie is firm to the touch.
6. Remove from the oven and allow to cool completely in the tin, then turn out on to a wire rack to cool. Cut into small squares to serve.

CHOCOLATE AND ORANGE MARMALADE COOKIES

These soft-textured biscuits are perfect with a cup of strong coffee. Do use good-quality plain chocolate and buy coarse-cut marmalade so that whenever you take a bite of biscuit you get a good bit of chewy marmalade or a piece of delicious chocolate. These are not sophisticated biscuits; they have a slightly rough texture and simply say 'eat me' so they will be appreciated by children – in fact, they are very easy to make so get the children to cook them for you.

These biscuits freeze well and will keep in an airtight container for several days.

Preparation time: 15 minutes
Cooking time: 12 minutes
Makes 16

110g/4oz butter
55g/2oz light brown sugar
grated zest of 1 large orange
225g/8oz plain chocolate, chopped

2 tablespoons coarse-cut Seville
   orange marmalade
170g/6oz self-raising flour

1. Preheat the oven to 180°C/350°F/gas mark 4. Line 2 baking sheets with bakewell paper.
2. Cream together the butter and sugar in a medium-sized bowl until light and fluffy. Add the orange zest.
3. Put 140g/5oz of the chocolate into a heatproof bowl set over, not in, a saucepan of simmering water. Allow it to melt without getting too hot, or the chocolate will become grainy.
4. Add the melted chocolate to the creamed butter and sugar. Stir in the marmalade and remaining chopped chocolate.
5. Fold in the flour and mix to a softish consistency.
6. Divide the mixture into 16 balls. Arrange the balls at least 5cm/2in apart on the baking sheets and press lightly into flatish rounds. Chill for 10 minutes.
7. Bake in the preheated oven for 10–12 minutes or until dry and smooth to touch. Leave to cool on the baking sheet for 5 minutes and then transfer to a wire rack to get completely cold.

ALMOND AND RAISIN FLAPJACKS

The variations possible on a flapjack are legion. We have enjoyed the following combinations – fig and walnut, date and pecan and apricot and chocolate. Flapjacks should be quite soft when they come out of the oven – they will harden considerably as they cool.

Preparation time: 10 minutes
Cooking time: 30 minutes

170g/6oz butter
110g/4oz soft light brown sugar
55g/2oz golden syrup
225g/8oz rolled oats

55g/2oz roasted almonds, roughly
 chopped
55g/2oz raisins

1. Preheat the oven to 190°C/375°F/gas mark 5. Grease a shallow baking tin.
2. Melt the butter.
3. Weigh out the sugar, then weigh the honey by spooning it on top of the sugar (thus preventing it from sticking to the scale pan) and add to the warm melted butter to heat through.
4. Remove the pan from the heat and stir in the oats, almonds and raisins.
5. Spread the mixture into the prepared tin.
6. Bake in the preheated oven for about 25 minutes until golden brown.
7. Remove from the oven, mark immediately into bars and leave to cool in the tin.

CHOCOLATE-CHIP MUFFINS

Making muffins is fun and easy. If you have a wire whisk, use it to stir the mixture but take care not to over-stir: muffins need no more than 12 strokes, or they become tough. Muffins are best eaten slightly warm. These can be frozen for up to a month and reheated in the oven or microwave.

Preparation time: 10 minutes
Baking time: 25 minutes
Makes 12

110g/4oz butter
110g/4oz soft light brown sugar
30g/1oz caster sugar
150ml/¼ pint milk
2 medium eggs, beaten

½ teaspoon vanilla essence
255g/9oz self-raising flour
½ teaspoon bicarbonate of soda
110g/4oz chocolate drops

1. Preheat the oven to 170°C/350°F/gas mark 4. Line 12 muffin tins with paper liners or with greaseproof paper discs and a thin coating of oil.
2. Melt the butter with the sugars. Allow to cool slightly.
3. Stir the milk into the butter and sugar mixture, then add the eggs and vanilla.
4. Sieve the flour and the bicarbonate of soda into a large bowl and make a well in the centre.
5. Quickly stir the wet ingredients into the flour with no more than 12 strokes, then fold in the chocolate drops.
6. Use a teacup to quickly ladle the mixture into the muffin tins. They should be almost full to the top.
7. Bake in the centre of the preheated oven for 25–30 minutes; a wooden skewer will come out clean of batter when they are done. For soft tops, cover with a teatowel to cool.

CHEESE AND BACON MUFFINS

When these muffins were tested at the school they were eaten in no time at all. They are absolutely delicious and perfect for breakfast. They can be baked in advance and then frozen. Defrost them slowly overnight in the fridge and then reheat in the oven or a microwave.

Cheese and bacon can be salty so be careful not to overseason with salt but do use plenty of pepper.

Preparation time: 15 minutes
Cooking time: 20–22 minutes
Makes 12

110g/4oz streaky bacon, diced
½ tablespoon oil
225g/8oz plain flour
½ teaspoon salt
2½ teaspoons baking powder

2 eggs
4 tablespoons olive oil
250ml/8fl oz full-fat milk
110g/4oz strong Cheddar cheese,
   coarsely grated

1. Preheat the oven to 190°C/375°F/gas mark 5. Oil 12 muffin tins or line with muffin cases.
2. Heat the oil in a frying pan, add the bacon and cook until it is golden brown and the fat has rendered. Remove from the pan with a slotted spoon and leave to drain on absorbent paper.

3. Sift the flour, salt and baking powder into a large bowl. In a separate bowl, beat together the eggs, oil and milk. Stir in the cheese and bacon.
4. Quickly stir the wet ingredients into the sifted flour. Spoon the batter into the muffin tins and bake for 20–25 minutes. Allow the muffins to cool for a few minutes in the tins before serving.

WAFFLES

Waffles are best made in a waffle iron but if you haven't got one they can be made like drop scones in a large metal frying pan. Waffles are particularly good served with very crisp thin American bacon and plenty of maple syrup.

Preparation time: 10 minutes
Cooking time: 2 minutes
Makes 18–20

3 eggs, separated
45g/1½oz unsalted butter, melted
few drops vanilla essence
340ml/12fl oz milk
340g/12oz plain flour
pinch of salt

2 teaspoons bicarbonate of soda
3 tablespoons icing sugar, plus
    extra for dusting

To serve
maple syrup

1. In a jug, mix together the egg yolks, melted butter, milk and vanilla essence.
2. Sift the flour, salt, bicarbonate of soda and sugar into a large mixing bowl. Make a well in the centre and gradually add the egg, butter and milk mixture.
3. Place the egg whites in a separate bowl and whisk to a medium peak. Using a large metal spoon, fold the egg whites into the batter.
4. Cook the waffles in a waffle iron according to the manufacturer's instructions.
5. Dust with more icing sugar and serve with maple syrup.

SODA BREAD

Soda bread is the traditional Irish breakfast loaf, served hot from the Aga with melted butter and jam. It is known as 'quickbread' because it doesn't involve the usual lengthy yeasted bread-making process or the use of bread flour, yet it still produces a delicious result – similar to a large scone.

This bread can be made with either plain white or wholemeal flour and it can be either sweet or savoury. The wholemeal version is ideal to serve with smoked salmon for a special breakfast. A sweet version can be made by adding currants, raisins or sultanas.

Preparation time: 10 minutes
Cooking time: 30 minutes

900g/2lb wholemeal flour, or
675g/1½lb wholemeal flour
and 225g/8oz plain white flour
2 teaspoons salt
2 teaspoons bicarbonate of soda
4 teaspoons cream of tartar
2 teaspoons sugar

45g/1½oz butter
570–860ml/1–1½ pints milk (if
using only wholemeal flour, the
recipe will need more liquid
than if made with a mixture of
2 flours)

1. Preheat the oven to 190°C/375°F/gas mark 5.
2. Sift the dry ingredients into a warmed large mixing bowl.
3. Rub in the butter and mix to a soft dough with the milk.
4. Shape with a minimum of kneading into a large circle about 5cm/2in thick. Dust lightly with flour. With the handle of a wooden spoon, make a cross on the top of the loaf; the dent should be 2cm/¾in deep.
5. Bake on a greased baking sheet in the preheated oven for 25–30 minutes. Allow to cool on a wire rack.

CHOCOLATE DROP SCONES

This is a simple variation of the traditional drop scone. The drop scones are fairly rich and should be served plain. It is important to use good quality chocolate.

Preparation time: 10 minutes
Cooking time: 20 minutes
Makes 30

225g/8oz self-raising flour
½ teaspoon salt
2 eggs, separated
290ml/½ pint milk

1 tablespoon butter, melted and
cooled
110g/4oz mixed white, plain and
milk chocolate, chopped, or
chocolate drops

1. Sift the flour into a large bowl.
2. Make a well in the centre of the mixture and add the egg yolks and a quarter of the milk.
3. Mix with a wooden spoon and gradually draw in the flour from the sides of the bowl making a smooth batter. Add the remaining milk gradually until the batter is the consistency of thick cream.
4. Fold in the melted butter and the chocolate.
5. Whisk the egg whites until stiff but not dry, then fold into the batter.
6. Meanwhile, lightly grease a heavy frying pan or griddle iron and heat it. When it is really hot, drop 2 spoonfuls of batter on to the surface, keeping them well separated.
7. Cook for 2–3 minutes. When the undersides of the scones are brown, bubbles rise to the surface. Using a fish slice, turn the scones over and brown the other side.
8. Keep warm, covered with a clean teatowel, until serving.

APRICOT AND GINGER SCONES

This recipe lifts a classic theme from the common or garden to the sublime. Ideal for a summer tea in the garden.

Preparation time: 25 minutes
Cooking time: 10 minutes
Makes 6

225g/8oz self-raising flour
½ teaspoon salt
55g/2oz butter
30g/1oz caster sugar
85g/3oz dried apricots, chopped
150ml/¼ pint milk
1 egg, beaten, to glaze

To serve
150ml/¼ pint double cream,
  lightly whipped
2 pieces stem ginger, finely
  chopped
2 tablespoons stem ginger syrup

1. Preheat the oven to 220°C/425°F/gas mark 7. Flour a baking sheet.
2. Sift the flour with the salt into a large bowl.
3. Rub in the butter until the mixture resembles breadcrumbs. Stir in the sugar, then add the apricots.
4. Make a deep well in the flour, pour in the milk and using a knife mix to a soft, spongy dough.
5. On a floured surface, knead the dough very lightly until it is just smooth. Roll or press out to about 2.5cm/1in thick and stamp into rounds with a small pastry cutter.
6. For a glossy crust, brush the scones with beaten egg; for a soft crust, sprinkle with flour; for a light gloss and soft crust, brush with milk.
7. Bake the scones at the top of the preheated oven for 7 minutes or until well risen and brown. Leave to cool on a wire rack or serve hot from the oven.
8. Stir the chopped ginger and ginger syrup into the whipped cream.
9. To serve: cut the scones horizontally in half and sandwich together with the ginger cream.

SPICED MINCEMEAT SCONES

These simple-to-make scones are ideal for Christmas and can be made using up mincemeat. They can be left to cool on a wire rack but are best served straight from the oven. They freeze well and only take about 1 hour to defrost.

Preparation time: 20 minutes
Cooking time: 10 minutes
Makes 10

225g/8oz self-raising flour, plus
   extra for dusting
1 teaspoon mixed spice
½ teaspoon salt
55g/2oz butter

15g/½oz caster sugar
150ml/¼ pint milk
4 tablespoons luxury mincemeat
1 egg, beaten, to glaze
demerara sugar

1. Preheat the oven to 220°C/420°F/gas mark 7. Dust a baking sheet with a little flour.
2. Sift the flour, mixed spice and salt into a large bowl.
3. Rub in the butter until the mixture resembles breadcrumbs. Stir in the sugar.
4. Make a deep well in the centre, pour in the milk, add the mincemeat, and using a knife, mix to a soft spongy dough.
5. On a floured surface, knead the dough very lightly until it is just smooth. Roll or press out to about 2.5cm/1in thick and stamp into rounds with a small pastry cutter.
6. Brush the scones with the beaten egg and sprinkle lightly with demerara sugar.
7. Bake the scones at the top of the preheated oven for 7 minutes or until well risen and brown.

MEDITERRANEAN SCONES

This recipe makes a large quantity of dough, but the scones can be baked and then frozen and used as required; they should be reheated before use. If you are in a hurry use a jar of suitable antipasta (drained) in place of the roast vegetables.

Preparation time: 10 minutes
Cooking time: 1–1½ hours
Makes 2 large

1 yellow pepper, sliced
1 red pepper, sliced
1 red onion, cut into
   1cm/½in slices
2 tablespoons olive oil
55g/2oz good-quality black olives,
   halved

450g/1lb self-raising flour
2 teaspoons salt
110g/4oz butter
290ml/½ pint milk

CAKES AND BISCUITS

1. Preheat oven to 220°C/425°F/gas mark 7.

2. Place the peppers and onion in a roasting tin and drizzle with the olive oil. Roast in the oven for 30–45 minutes until the vegetables are soft. Allow to cool.

3. Sift the flour and salt into a large bowl. Rub in the butter until the mixture resembles breadcrumbs. Add the vegetables and olives.

4. Add the milk and stir together to a smooth dough.

5. Cut out into thick scones or leave as two large ones. Place on a baking sheet.

6. Bake at the top of the preheated oven. The small scones will take about 10 minutes to cook and large ones will take up to 45 minutes.

7. Leave to cool slightly on a wire rack but serve them while still warm.

MISCELLANEOUS

PLUM AND ORANGE CHUTNEY

Chutneys are the easiest preserves to make. They are mixtures, always sweet and sour, somewhere between a pickle and a jam. They are generally made of fruit, or sometimes soft vegetables. Chutneys improve with keeping and, if they are bottled correctly, can be eaten for up to 2 years. It is important to make sure that the jam jars used for bottling are sterilised. The easiest way to do this is to wash the jars and lids thoroughly, and then heat them in a low oven (100°C/200°F/ gas mark ½) until dry. Pour the hot chutney into the jars, cover with a waxed jam cover disc (or a greaseproof paper circle soaked in vodka!), pushed right on top of the hot chutney, and seal with a tight-fitting lid or cellophane jam cover and elastic band. (Cellophane covers are sold in supermarkets and chemists in packets with the waxed jam covers.) This quantity of chutney should fill 2 × 1lb jars.

Preparation time: 30 minutes
Cooking time: 1 hour 45 minutes
Makes 2 × 450g/1lb jars

450g/1lb cooking apples, peeled, cored and chopped
450g/1lb onions, peeled and finely chopped
450g/1lb plums, stoned and chopped
1 clove garlic, peeled and finely chopped

2 teaspoons yellow mustard seeds
1 stick cinnamon
1 star anise
290ml/½ pint cider vinegar
85g/3oz soft light brown sugar
85/3oz soft dark brown sugar
zest and juice of 1 orange

1. Put all the ingredients, except for the sugar and the orange zest and juice, into a small saucepan and simmer gently, stirring occasionally, for 1 hour, or until the mixture is soft and the liquid has almost evaporated.

2. Add the sugar and orange zest and juice and stir over a low heat until the sugar has dissolved.
3. Bring to the boil and boil rapidly, stirring, until thick.
4. Remove the cinnamon stick and star anise, pour into sterilised dry jars and cover as described above.

DATE CHUTNEY

This sweet and sour chutney is not only the perfect accompaniment to a spicy meal – it also tastes delicious in cheese sandwiches.

170ml/6fl oz malt vinegar *fresh root ginger*
3 tablespoons brown sugar *30g/1oz sultanas*
140g/5oz dried dates, chopped *1 teaspoon paprika*
2 cloves garlic, finely chopped *salt*

1. Put the vinegar and sugar into a saucepan and bring slowly to the boil. Stir until the sugar has dissolved. Lower the heat and add the dates, garlic and ginger. Cook over a low heat for 15 minutes, stirring continuously. Add the sultanas, paprika and salt to taste and cook for a further 5 minutes.
2. Put into jars and store. Once opened, keep refrigerated for up to a month.

Biographical Note

Leith's School of Food and Wine was established in 1975 to provide professional training for career cooks and short courses for amateurs. The school provides comprehensive theoretical and practical teaching, qualifying students to enter the highly competitive food and wine business and begin a rewarding career. There is a commitment to classical techniques and methods but with a fresh and modern approach. The guiding principle of the teaching at Leith's School is to impart enthusiasm for the trade and instil a lasting love of good food and wine in students.

Caroline Waldegrave is the co-owner and Principal of Leith's School of Food and Wine. She joined the catering company Leith's Good Food in 1971 as a cook, after training at the Cordon Bleu Cookery School in London. She has written and co-authored numerous cookery books, among them *Leith's Cookery Course*, *Leith's Cookery Bible*, *Leith's Cookery School*, *Leith's Easy Dinner Parties* and *Leith's Fish Bible*.

Leith's School of Food and Wine Ltd
21 St Alban's Grove
London W8 5BP
Tel: 020-7229-0177
Email: info@leiths.com
Website: www.leiths.com

INDEX